MONTANA

JOE MONTANA WITH DICK SCHAAP

Turner Publishing, Inc.

ATLANTA

AN OPUS BOOK

To Jennifer—generous and loving, supportive and strong—who has given of herself to help me realize my dreams.
To our kids—Alexandra, Elizabeth, Nathaniel, and Nicholas—for being there for me to come home to.
And to Mom and Dad, who sacrificed so that I would have a chance to play football
and taught me the values that set me on my way.

Library of Congress Cataloging-in-Publication Data
Montana, Joe, 1956–
    Montana/by Joe Montana with Dick Schaap.
       p.   cm.
    ISBN 1-57036-236-X (hardcover)
    ISBN 1-57036-240-8 (paperback)
       1. Montana, Joe, 1956– .   2. Football players—United States—Biography.
       I. Schaap, Dick, 1934– . II. Title

GV939. M59A3   1995
796.332'092—dc20
[B]   95-24003
                                                                          CIP

Produced by Opus Productions Inc., 300 West Hastings Street
Vancouver, British Columbia, Canada V6B 1K6

Published by Turner Publishing, Inc.
A Subsidiary of Turner Broadcasting System, Inc.
1050 Techwood Drive, N.W.
Atlanta, Georgia 30318

Film and separations through PrintNet at Digital PrePress International
Printed and bound in the U.S.A. by Inland Press

10 9 8 7 6 5 4 3 2 1

TABLE OF CONTENTS

High school days: Joe Montana's first starting assignment for the Ringgold Rams, Saturday, September 30, 1972.

He was Joe Cool, the quarterback who never quit, the quarterback who could overcome any deficit, any pressure, any injury.

Once, Joe Montana led his team to victory after trailing by twenty-eight points at halftime.

More than once, Montana led his team to victory after trailing by fourteen points in the fourth quarter.

Thirty-one times, Montana led his team to victory after trailing in the fourth quarter, and more than three-fourths of those trademark comebacks took place on the road, heroics in front of hostile crowds.

Four times in four appearances in the brightest spotlight, Montana led his team to victory in the Super Bowl.

Once, Montana ruptured a spinal disk so severely he needed two hours of back surgery to salvage his career. Eight weeks later, he returned to the starting lineup and led his team to victory.

Five years later, Montana tore a tendon in his right elbow, his throwing elbow, endured two operations and did not start a game for two seasons. His first game back in the starting lineup, he completed the first nine passes he threw and led his team to victory.

He was, above all else, a winner. He won more than seventy per cent of the games he started during an illustrious sixteen-year career in the National Football League, a career that started inauspiciously: Eighty-one players were picked ahead of him in the 1979 draft.

But if the tangible evidence of Joe Montana's greatness is overwhelming, the intangibles are even more impressive: the way he transmitted his calm and his concentration to his teammates, the way he inspired them to their finest performances, the way he shrugged off repeated poundings and high praise with equal grace.

He was a superstar without a superego, as unassuming as he was unflappable, never strutting, never preening, never guaranteeing a victory or trashing an opponent, always sharing the credit for his success with his teammates. Some gifted athletes speak of themselves endlessly in the first person—"I, I, I … " Others prefer the third person—"Bo, Bo, Bo … " Joe Montana is the rarest of athletes, one who tends to speak of himself in the second person—"You do this, and you do that … "

On the field, crouching behind massive linemen, Montana often appeared slight, even fragile, but he is six-foot-two, or almost, and close to 200 pounds, sturdy enough to withstand the collisions of his craft, athletic enough to dunk a basketball.

Off the field, Joe Montana is delightful company, a connoisseur of good wine and good food, a proud husband and father, a man whose youthful good looks are reinforced by a shy, winning smile, a private man who is polite to his public. He anticipates attention, but seems embarrassed and even surprised by it, comprehends what he has achieved, but is not overly impressed by it.

In other words, Joe Montana is everything the subject of a biography in pictures should be—remarkably photogenic and stunningly gifted—except one: He hates to blow his own horn. But even with that one instrument muted, or at least tempered, I suspect the music of Montana comes through loud and clear.

DICK SCHAAP
New York City
1995

**"To me, it was just another episode of Montana magic.
He put the ball exactly where he had to."**
DWIGHT CLARK, TEAMMATE, 49ERS

Legendary pigskin: The football Dwight Clark caught on the edge of his fingertips to make "The Catch."

In the history of professional football, only a handful of defining plays have transformed and elevated the sport.

1958: Baltimore Colts vs. the New York Giants for the National Football League Championship. Eight minutes into sudden-death overtime, inside the Giants' ten-yard line, Colts' quarterback John Unitas elected to pass. He connected at the one-yard line, setting up the touchdown plunge that ended what many call the greatest game ever played. "Weren't you taking a chance, risking an interception?" Unitas was asked after the game. "When you know what you're doing," he replied, "you're not going to be intercepted."

1967: The "Ice Bowl." Green Bay Packers vs. the Dallas Cowboys for the NFL Championship and a berth in Super Bowl II. On fourth and a yard to go for a touchdown, trailing Dallas 17-14 in the closing seconds, Packers' quarterback Bart Starr bent over in the huddle and coolly said, "Thirty-one wedge. I'll carry the ball." Behind Jerry Kramer blocking Jethro Pugh, Starr squeezed into the end zone for the game-winning touchdown.

1968: New York Jets vs. the Oakland Raiders for the American Football League Championship. In the fourth-quarter drive that lifted the Jets to victory, Joe Namath threw a pass that traveled close to seventy yards into the arms of Don Maynard, who was brought down on the Raiders' six-yard line. On the next play, Namath hit Maynard for a touchdown. Two weeks later, the Jets shocked Baltimore in Super Bowl III.

And then there was The Catch, the perfect end to another perfect drive, engineered by a quarterback who had a touch of Unitas's brashness, Starr's intelligence, and Namath's courage. It was, in a very real sense, the play that spawned the legend of Joe Montana.

When I woke up on Sunday, January 10, 1982, in the Hyatt hotel in Burlingame, not far from the San Francisco airport, I turned to my roommate, Dwight Clark, and I said, "Dwight, this afternoon I'm going to throw a touchdown pass to you in the last minute of the game to beat the Dallas Cowboys and put us in the Super Bowl."

"Just don't throw it too high," Dwight Clark said.

Maybe that's the way the day began. But I don't think so. The truth is, Dwight and I never used to talk much about football on Sunday mornings. And that morning, I was concentrating too hard on the Dallas Cowboys.

They were America's Team. They had been a winning team for sixteen straight seasons. They had played in five Super Bowls in the 1970s. They had Tony Dorsett in their backfield (we were in high school at the same time in Western Pennsylvania, but we never played against each other) and they had Randy White in their line, as strong and quick and mean as any lineman who ever lived. They also had Too Tall Jones and Harvey Martin in the defensive line, guys who seemed to end up in the Pro Bowl every year.

We were San Francisco's team. We thought we were pretty good, too. We had the best record in the NFL going into the National Conference championship game against the Cowboys, fourteen victories and three defeats. Pretty remarkable considering that we had lost two of our first three games, and that the year before we were 6-10, and the year before that, my rookie year, we were 2-14. The 49ers had never won a Super Bowl, had never even played in one. The last three times they'd gotten into the playoffs, they'd been knocked out each time by the Dallas Cowboys.

We didn't have one player on our team who'd ever played in a Pro Bowl, but we had some guys who were going to play in a lot of them: Ronnie Lott and Dwight Hicks on defense and Randy Cross and Dwight Clark on offense. We'd played Dallas during the regular season, and we'd beaten them badly. Still, before the NFC championship game, the Cowboys acted like they were the favorites. Like we didn't have a chance, we were just lucky to be there. Too Tall Jones, especially. He claimed he had no respect for us.

We were all pumped up for the game.

On one early play, Too Tall Jones came tearing after me, and I faked to the outside. He took the fake, and when I pulled up, he fell down. I threw a thirty-eight-yard pass to Dwight Clark. "Respect that!" I yelled at Too Tall, who was a former professional heavyweight boxer. I didn't mean to yell, but I had to. The crowd was making a lot of noise.

Keith Fahnhorst, our tackle, shouted back at me: "Settle down, Joe. You're getting them worked up and they're taking it out on me."

Later on in the second quarter, Harvey Martin sacked me, and as he stood over me, he said, "I will be back." I couldn't help it. I had to have a comeback, and it had to be on the same wavelength. So I said, "Well, I hope so, because I was beginning to think you weren't in the game."

Randy Cross, who was trying his best to protect me from the Cowboys, wasn't too happy with me for that. "Joe, shut the hell up and just play," Randy advised me.

Maybe we were too pumped up. We weren't playing all that well. Six turnovers—three fumbles, and I had thrown three interceptions. You don't usually win when you have six turnovers. But we were losing by only six points, 27-21, when we got the ball on our own eleven-yard line with four minutes and fifty-four seconds to play in the fourth quarter.

Plenty of time to go eighty-nine yards.

Bill Walsh, our coach, and his assistants could see that we had time, and they saw that the Cowboys were using six defensive backs, only five men up front. We could run the ball. Lenvil Elliott, a veteran at thirty years old (I thought that was old—then), carried the ball four or five times and gained good yardage every time.

Strategy session: Joe Montana, Dwight Clark, and Mike Shumann discuss how to shake Dallas coverage.

With two minutes left in the game, we were just across midfield. Forty-nine yards from a touchdown, and we were running out of gas. Randy Cross, one of several guys who'd been fighting the flu all week, threw up on the field, right in the huddle. I wouldn't even have noticed if someone hadn't asked him, "What the hell do you want to do that here for?"

Randy apologized. "I couldn't help it," he said.

During the two-minute timeout, on the sidelines, Bill Walsh asked me, "What do you think of Freddie Solomon on a reverse left?"

I hesitated. I wasn't sure it would work. Then I said, "Okay, I'll block the defensive end."

The defensive end on that side was Harvey Martin. I knew he'd be glad to see me coming at him. I figured I'd just throw myself at his knees. But when we called the play, Martin went upfield, and I found myself looking at Randy White. I had tried to block him the last time we played the Cowboys, and when I'd hit him, he had just started laughing. This time, at least, I sort of collided with him, chest high, just enough to slow him down a little.

Freddie Solomon ran for fourteen yards. Then I got lucky. I threw a pass I thought Everson Walls would knock down. He'd already intercepted me twice. But this time he just grazed the ball; Dwight Clark caught it, and we were on the twenty-five-yard line.

Don't think I remember all this, yard for yard. I don't. I was only thinking about the goal line. The record book reminds me that Freddie Solomon then caught a pass and we were on the thirteen-yard line with a minute and fifteen seconds to play. We called a timeout. Dwight collapsed on the ground. "You all right?" the trainer asked him.

"Maybe we were too pumped up.
We weren't playing all that well.
Six turnovers—three fumbles,
and I had thrown three interceptions.
You don't usually win when
you have six turnovers."
JOE MONTANA

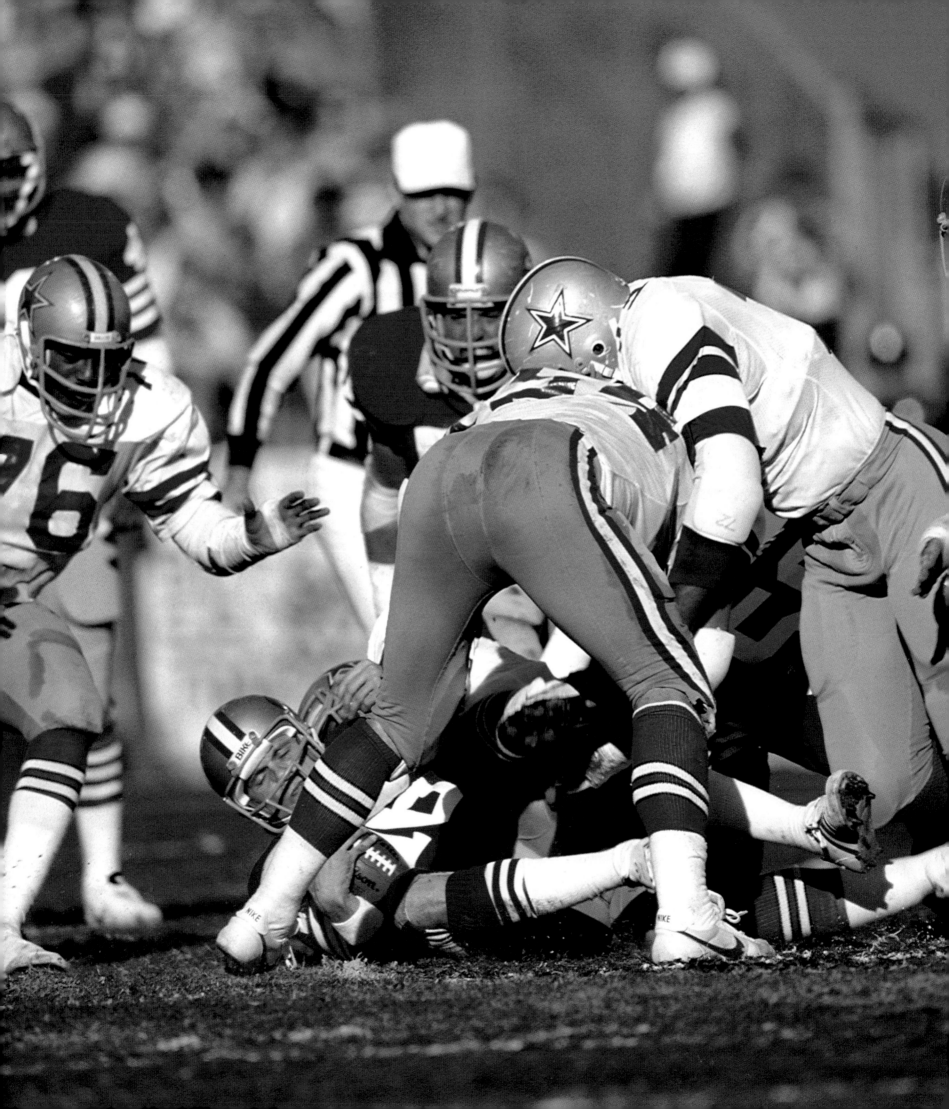

"When you're behind, the idea is to do something, but not everything. You want to get a flow going, then you can take a chance. You want to go through every situation ahead of time." JOE MONTANA

Half-time, Dallas 17–San Francisco 14:
A moment of introspection, prelude to greatness.

"Water! Gimme some water," Dwight managed to say. He'd had the flu all week, too.

Dwight and I had been roommates from the first day of training camp in 1979, our rookie year. He was a tenth-round draft choice from Clemson (I kept reminding him who won the Notre Dame–Clemson game when we were juniors) and he hadn't caught very many passes in college.

He didn't think he had a chance of making the 49ers. Every morning, when we went to breakfast, we had to walk past John McVay, who was in charge of player personnel, and if he said, "Bill wants to see you," you knew you were gone, you were going to be cut. Dwight was scared to death he was going to hear, "Bill wants to see you." I was pretty sure I was going to make the team—Steve DeBerg was the only quarterback in camp with any real experience—but every morning I acted like I was scared, too, just to keep Dwight company. After a while, we started sneaking into breakfast the back way, so we wouldn't have to pass John McVay.

Dwight would stay out after practice every day, catching and catching and catching, trying to make up, I guess, for all the passes he didn't catch in college. I'd throw to him, and so would the other quarterbacks. His hard work paid off. He made the team, and by the next season, 1980, he was a starter and one of the best receivers in the league.

Dwight had that uncanny knack of being able to find a hole in the defense. When you were in trouble, he was always trying to come back to help you. He never stopped working. Any receiver who does that, you always end up looking for him. You owe it to him. You know he's going to find a way to get open.

Now, with seventy-five seconds to play, and at least half our guys ready to die, Coach Walsh called a pass to Solomon. Freddie got open, but I missed him. Second down. Lenvil carried the ball down to the six-yard line. Third and three. We called time out with fifty-eight seconds to go.

"Sprint right option," Coach Walsh told me.

Right from the beginning of training camp, we'd been polishing this play. Every time we worked on our goal-line or short-yardage offense, we practiced "Sprint right option."

Dwight Clark was flanked out to the right. Freddie Solomon was in the slot to Dwight's left. Dwight was supposed to cut to his left. Freddie was to cut under Dwight, to the right, to the corner, and if Clark picked off the defense, then Freddie would be open in the corner. If Freddie wasn't open, then, as I moved to my right, I'd look for Dwight, who was the secondary receiver. His job, after he ran his initial route, was to stop in the back of the end zone and work down the end line. My job was to throw the ball to him and throw it high. High enough so that if he couldn't reach up and grab it, the ball would sail out of bounds and we would still have another play.

We called the play, and I started to my right, and I looked for Freddie, saw he was covered, then looked for Dwight. Too Tall Jones and a couple of his friends were coming at me. I wasn't going to take the sack. Not then. Not with fourth down coming up. I couldn't see if Dwight was open, but I knew where he'd be—we'd done it so many times. Off-balance, my left foot off the ground, I let the ball go.

When the ball leaves your hand, you usually kind of know where it's going. Knees, waist, numbers—you can sense it. This time I thought it was going to be just where Dwight could reach up and catch it. Not too difficult. That was my perception.

Then I got knocked down, and I didn't see the ball get to Dwight. I didn't see him jump, and I didn't see him catch the ball. But I heard it. I heard the touchdown. I heard it from the San Francisco fans, who were screaming. I heard it from one of the Cowboys (I don't know which one), who said to me, disgusted, "You just beat America's team."

I was wiped out, but I didn't miss a beat. I was still angry with the Cowboys. "You can sit at home with the rest of America," I said, "and watch the Super Bowl in two weeks."

When I got to the sidelines, everyone was yelling, "Dwight made a great catch! Dwight made a great catch!" I thought it couldn't have been that great. When I asked how high the ball had been, and somebody told me, I didn't believe it.

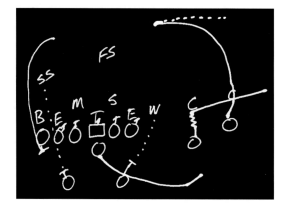

Sprint right option:
The play Coach Bill Walsh called to set up
"The Catch." Diagram drawn by Montana.

Ray Wersching kicked the extra point that put us ahead, 28-27, with fifty-one seconds to play. Then our defense stopped the Cowboys' final drive. Suddenly, we were the champions of the NFC. We were going to the Super Bowl.

We had used up everything we had. Physically and emotionally, we were drained. We screamed and yelled, and when we got to the locker room we collapsed. I lay on the floor under the water fountain. I couldn't get up till our equipment manager, Chico Norton, helped me.

Then Irv Cross from CBS interviewed Dwight and me together. When he showed us the replay of the winning touchdown, I finally got to see just how high Dwight leaped to make the catch. At six-foot-four, he just got the ball on the edge of his fingertips and managed to bring it down.

The play has always been called The Catch, and that's just what it was. The Catch. It wasn't a bad pass—I wasn't throwing it away; Dwight said it was a perfect pass, any lower and Walls would have batted it away—but it sure wasn't The Pass.

The Catch got us into our first Super Bowl, and two weeks later we beat Cincinnati for our first Super Bowl victory. Eight years later, we'd won four of them.

What would've happened if that pass had been a couple of inches higher? If Dwight hadn't been able to catch it?

Some people say it was the turning point, that it changed everything for us. I don't know. I believe we would have scored on the next play.

I never thought we were going to lose. Not that day. Not any day. Not ever.

per trying to get the ball to Dwight high, so no one else could get it. I never saw the catch. I heard the crowd roar." JO

"Exuberant kid who had stardom written all over him,
but nobody ever resented it because it came naturally."

CARL CRAWLEY, COACH, LITTLE WILDCATS

Joe Montana was born in New Eagle and raised in Monongahela, gritty blue-collar towns on the outskirts of Pittsburgh in Western Pennsylvania, an ethnically diverse region known for its mines and its mills and its quarterbacks. The mines and the mills have suffered in recent years, economic victims of a diminishing demand for steel and coal, but the quarterbacks have flourished. George Blanda was born in Youngwood, Pa., John Unitas in Pittsburgh, Joe Namath in Beaver Falls, and all three escaped from the mines and the mills and wound up, instead, in the Pro Football Hall of Fame. Dan Marino of the Miami Dolphins and Jim Kelly of the Buffalo Bills both were born in Pittsburgh and forged in Western Pennsylvania's red-hot football crucible, and both of them might also end up in the Hall of Fame. They would be inducted sometime after Joe Montana, of course.

What is it that has caused so many gifted quarterbacks to thrive in this small section of the country? It is, most likely, the spirit, the fiercely competitive spirit of first- and second-generation Americans, Serbs and Croats, Slavs and Greeks, Irish and Italian, struggling to survive and then to win. Even pick-up softball games in towns like Monongahela and Beaver Falls and Aliquippa are played for blood, cousins against cousins, brothers against brothers. They play fair, but they play hard, and no one likes to lose. Joe Montana clearly shares that spirit.

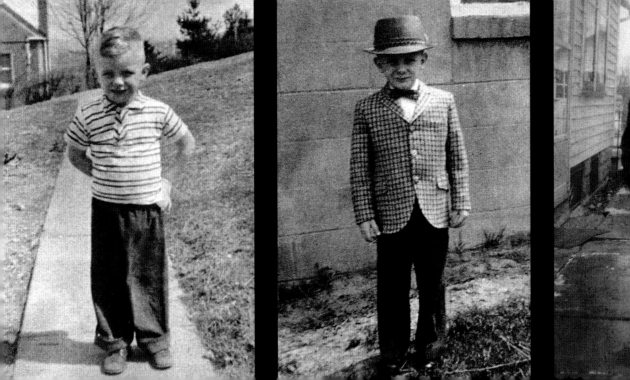

When I was starting to play sports, I really didn't know about the Pennsylvania quarterback tradition. I knew who Joe Namath was—he won the Super Bowl when I was a twelve-year-old playing quarterback in the Pop Warner league—and I liked him, but he wasn't my idol. I admired Len Dawson, too, and the Kansas City Chiefs, and, of course, when I was in high school, the Pittsburgh Steelers were building the team that won four Super Bowls. Terry Bradshaw and Lynn Swann and John Stallworth and Franco Harris. When I wasn't pretending I was Namath or Dawson, I was pretending I was Bradshaw.

Even though I lived only a few miles from Pittsburgh, I never went to a Steelers game. In fact, I never saw a pro football game live until I played in one. I was too busy playing ball to watch it. I played everything—football and baseball and basketball—365 days a year. It was what you did in Mon City, which is what we called Monongahela. In the summers, I'd play one, sometimes two baseball games a day, and still find time to play in outdoor basketball leagues. I must have played more basketball than anything else, because it was easier to get a game. All you needed was a ball and you could play in the schoolyard or the gym. You didn't have to pull a bunch of guys together like you did for football.

I wasn't particularly big or particularly strong, pretty much average size, but I guess I had a knack for sports. I'm told that my grandfather Joe used to tell my grandmother that I was special, that I was going to be good, but I don't remember him ever telling me. My father Joe used to play ball with me and coach me all the time. Even when I was a little kid, not even ten years old, Dad would have me throw a football through a swinging tire. You learn accuracy, and you learn timing. You throw to where you know the tire is going to be. Like Dwight Clark swinging back through the end zone.

My father and I played all sports together, but basketball was his best game. He had played in the Navy, and he didn't like to lose. He grabbed. He pushed. He threw his elbows around. He was the kind of guy who would step on your foot if you tried to go around him. Or trip you as you went by. I learned his tricks. I didn't like to lose, either.

Baseball, I pitched and I played shortstop, or filled in anywhere. I threw a few no-hitters in Little League. In high school, I would swing for the fences, but I wasn't a home-run hitter. I wanted to be, but I wasn't. I was a home-run hitter without power. Pitching, I threw a fastball and a curve; that was it. I didn't throw a screwball, even though that's basically the motion you use—twisting your wrist to the left, counterclockwise—when you're throwing a football, throwing a spiral.

"I played all sports in the service, but when I was a kid I never had anyone to take me in the backyard and throw a ball to me. Maybe that's why I got Joe started in sports. Once he got started, he was always waiting at the door with a ball when I came home from work. He loved it so much, and I loved watching him. And I wanted to make sure he learned the right way." JOE MONTANA, SR.

My father got me into organized football when I was eight years old, with a Pop Warner team called the Monongahela Little Wildcats. You were supposed to be nine to play in the league, but somehow he got me started when I was eight. My first coach was a man named Carl Crawley, and I was lucky. He was one of the best Pop Warner coaches I could imagine. He knew football; he later became a college football official, and worked some of the major bowl games. More important, he knew kids. He had "kid skills." Not "people skills," kid skills—they're different. You have to be more patient with kids, and he was. He cared about you, and he disciplined you at the same time. He didn't overplay winning, but he stressed it. You wanted to win for him as well as for yourself. Carl Crawley and his wife and my parents were the closest of friends. My Dad was like a full-time part-time coach with the Little Wildcats.

Even then I liked the games a lot better than practice. I especially hated wind sprints. Not as much as one of my friends did. His name was Tank, which tells you something about his size. He was always fighting the weight limit in Pop Warner football; I think it was 130 or 132 pounds. Most of the time, when the rest of us practiced, Tank ran laps, trying to lose weight. I kind of like that idea of a weight limit. I wish they'd had it in the NFL. If they'd had a 225-pound

weight limit, say, something Reggie White or Lawrence Taylor couldn't get down to, I might still be playing.

When I was ten, I decided for the first time I wanted to quit playing football. It sounds funny now, but I felt like my whole life had been sports, all ten years of it, and I wanted to try something else. I wanted to join the Cub Scouts. My cousins were in the Cub Scouts, and I thought that might be more fun than playing football. At first, my Dad told me it was okay to quit football. Then he thought about it and he told me, "I don't want you to quit something you've started, or it could become a habit. You finish the season, and then you can quit football." By the time the season ended, I had forgotten all about the Cub Scouts.

Later, my cousins, the same ones who had been Cub Scouts, held different jobs, and I wanted to get one, too. Maybe work in a gas station, make some money while I was in high school. But my parents told me that as long as I played sports, I wouldn't have to work, that they would see that I had everything I needed. Not everything I *wanted*. Everything I *needed*. My parents both worked for a finance company—my father was the office manager, and my mother handled the accounts. They didn't make a lot of money—we lived from check to check most of the time—but they made sure I always had what I needed.

"There was no show-off in him. He wanted to win, and he'd do whatever it took. With Joe on the field, the other kids knew they were never out of any game."

CARL CRAWLEY, COACH, LITTLE WILDCATS

The making of a three-time Super Bowl MVP. Above: *The Monongahela Peanut League All Stars. (Montana is far right, back row.)* Below: *The Monongahela Pop Warner League's Little Wildcats. (Montana is fourth from right, back row.)*

We had good teams in high school. They had combined two high schools, one in Monongahela and one in Donora, into Ringgold High School. Both schools had strong athletic traditions. Stan Musial came from Donora, and so did the Griffeys, Ken Senior and Ken Junior. In fact, I played baseball with the older Griffey's younger brother, Junior's uncle.

The two high schools had been bitter rivals for a long time. Then, suddenly, not long before I got there, they were one team representing two separate campuses, one in Donora, the other in Monongahela. The campus in Donora was predominantly black, the one in Monongahela predominantly white. The players on the teams got along fine—race was no big deal to us. We joked about it, that was all. But there was tension between the towns and between the students. There was an ugly stabbing incident while I was in school, and we had security guards all over the Monongahela campus.

I never got into trouble as a kid, hardly ever even had a fight. I didn't have time. I was too busy playing ball. I had to get my schoolwork done, too. My parents made sure of that. I do wish I had worked harder on it then. Most kids don't realize if you work harder early on, it makes it much, much easier when you get to college. You learn when to study and how to study. I was passing all my subjects, I was getting decent grades, but I was really concentrating on sports.

Football hero and senior class vice president, Ringgold High School, 1973.

In high school football, the coach I was closest to was Jeff Petrucci, who handled the quarterbacks and went on to coach in small colleges. Petrucci had played quarterback in college and understood the game and the position. He understood the things that went wrong, why they went wrong, and how you deal with them. That really set a good foundation for me.

The head coach was Chuck Abramski, who was a wild man—he used to hit kids over the helmet with his clipboard—but the things he did for the kids far outweighed everything else. When he arrived, the equipment was dreadful. He upgraded it, saw to it that we got better and safer helmets and shoulder pads. Whether you were one of his stars or one of his scrubs, he did everything he could to get you into college. He wrote letters, he made phone calls, he used all his contacts. He wanted to get everybody a scholarship. He wanted to see the kids get an education, and he wanted to take the financial burden off the parents.

Coach Abramski didn't make me the starting quarterback till my junior year. He had me playing behind a friend of mine named Paul Timko when I was a sophomore, till he switched Timko to tight end. His first game at tight end, I threw Paul four touchdown passes—I wanted to keep him happy there. I was happy at quarterback. I made the *Parade* All-American team my senior year, and a lot of colleges were interested in me.

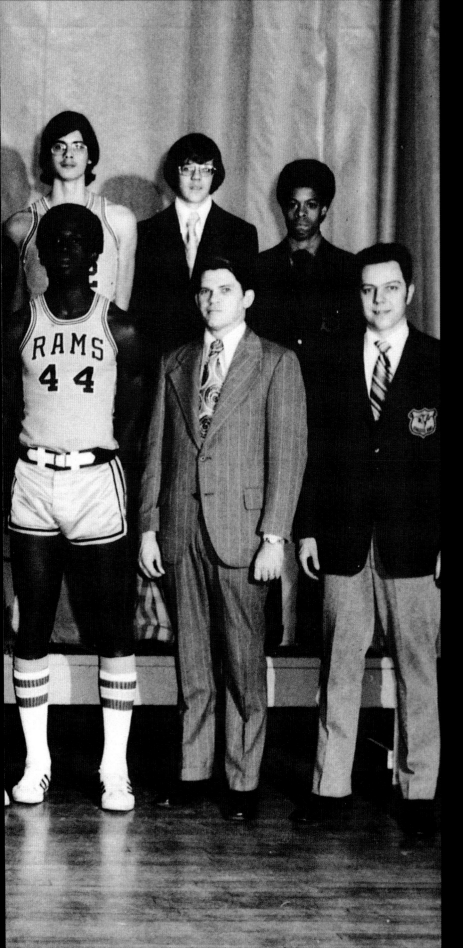

"As a senior in high school I wasn't sure really what I wanted to do. I was kind of divided between basketball and football. I remember a conversation with my father in the car one day... I said I had made up my mind, and I knew where I was going to go and he said, 'I already know, too.' He thought I was going to take the easy road out and go and play basketball. I had already made up my mind to play football at Notre Dame at that point." JOE MONTANA

Above: *Ringgold Rams booster pin handcrafted by Joe's No. 1 fan, Theresa Montana*

Left: *Ringgold Rams were the 1972-73 Western Pennsylvania basketball champions and runners-up for the state championship. (Montana is second player from left, front row.)*

"Joe had natural ability.
Joe could beat you at
ping-pong, he could beat
you at pool, he could beat
you at tennis. He was a
great putter, and of course
a great basketball player,
a pitcher and shortstop.
He had all the abilities it
takes to be a winner."

CHUCK ABRAMSKI, HEAD COACH,
RINGGOLD HIGH SCHOOL

*Awarded to Ringgold High's finest:
Cut-out trophies of Montana
in his Rams football and
basketball uniforms.*

Montana's 1974 signing of a letter of intent to play football at Notre Dame made the local paper. Seated with Joe are his parents, Theresa and Joe, Sr.; standing are (left) Ringgold High basketball coach Fran LaMendola and (right) football coach Chuck Abramski.

I was most interested in Notre Dame. I'd been hearing about Notre Dame all my life. My father was a Notre Dame fan and he wanted me to go there. I'd watch their games on TV on Saturday afternoon, or if I was playing Saturday afternoon, I'd watch the Notre Dame network Sunday mornings. I didn't miss many of their games. Terry Hanratty was my favorite when I was in Pop Warner football. On many of those Saturday afternoons I used to pretend I was Hanratty, passing to Jim Seymour.

I set up recruiting visits to Notre Dame, Michigan State, Georgia, Minnesota, and Penn State. My Dad liked Penn State—that was the only reason I considered them. Joe Paterno always tried to turn high school quarterbacks into college linebackers: I wonder, would he've been able to do that with me? I kind of liked Pitt—Johnny Majors was the coach, and Tony Dorsett was there—but I thought it was too close to Monongahela. It would've been like staying at home.

I didn't visit any of the schools that offered me basketball scholarships, but I could've gone to North Carolina State, which won the national championship my senior year in high school. I would've been a freshman when David Thompson,

their great All-American, was a senior; I would've played in the backcourt with him.

Actually, I had a choice between N.C. State, the national champions in basketball, and Notre Dame, the national champions in football. I took my recruiting trip to Notre Dame in January 1974, and my host was a guy named Frank Allocco, a back-up quarterback on the championship team. He was very honest. He told me not to go to Notre Dame, I'd hate it. "It's a great place with a great football tradition," he said, "but it's not a lot of fun. Go somewhere else and you can have fun."

The weather was miserable the whole weekend I visited the campus in South Bend, Indiana, but we did manage to get out to a Notre Dame basketball game. They were playing UCLA, which featured Bill Walton and two or three other All-Americans. UCLA had won eighty-eight games in a row, which was a college record. Notre Dame ended the streak, beating UCLA by one point. It was a pretty good game.

Despite Allocco's advice, and despite the weather, I decided to attend Notre Dame, so I cancelled my other recruiting trips. I was going to go play for Ara Parseghian, one of the great coaches in the history of football.

**"Anyone who says he saw Joe Montana in high school—or even in college—
and knew he was going to be a great quarterback in the NFL is lying."**

ARA PARSEGHIAN, COACH, NOTRE DAME

A fabled chapter in a winning tradition: Montana's battle-worn Fighting Irish headgear.

Notre Dame may mean Our Lady in French, but in the United States, it means football. Winning football. Its tradition dates back at least to 1910, the year the Fighting Irish began a streak of twenty-seven games without defeat, a streak that included a 1913 victory over West Point, notable because it popularized a startling new weapon—the forward pass.

Notre Dame is the only major college team that has won more than seventy-five per cent of its games, a record that spans more than one hundred seasons, and the only school that has won eight national championships since the start of the Associated Press poll in 1936. Home to the two most successful coaches in major college football history—Knute Rockne and Frank Leahy—it has also groomed more Heisman Trophy winners than any other school—Angelo Bertelli, John Lujack, Leon Hart, John Lattner, Paul Hornung, John Huarte, and Tim Brown—and more unanimous All-Americans, twenty-nine of them.

Notre Dame's most famous players include George Gipp, "The Gipper," portrayed in film by future president Ronald Reagan, and "The Four Horsemen," who, as Grantland Rice wrote, "are known in dramatic lore as Famine, Pestilence, Destruction and Death. Those are only aliases. Their real names are Stuhldreher, Miller, Crowley, and Layden." All four Horsemen are in the College Football Hall of Fame, joining thirty-one other Notre Dame players, an unmatched delegation. But, surprisingly, only four Notre Dame players—Hornung, Wayne Millner, George Connor, and Alan Page—have gone on to the Pro Football Hall of Fame.

Set against this glittering background, it is remarkable that the best-known player ever to emerge from Notre Dame is a man who barely played during his first three years there—a man named Joe Montana.

A few years ago, I invited my grandmother to join Jennifer and the kids and me on a trip to Sicily, where Gram had been born. She thanked me, but said no; she wanted to remember it the way it was when she was growing up. I feel the same way about Notre Dame. I haven't been back there since I graduated. I hear it's grown tenfold, and there are lots of big new buildings. But I like to remember it as a small place.

I also remember it as a place where I struggled and where I grew, where I faced frustrations in the classroom and on the football field, and where I made good friends. Nick DeCicco was my roommate. His father, Mike, was the fencing coach and the academic advisor to the football team; his grandfather fed us home-cooked Italian meals. Mark Ewald was my best friend; he was on the basketball team we had that won the intramural Bookstore Tournament, which is a pretty big deal at Notre Dame. Mark was a football player, too, but when he realized he wasn't going to play much, he just decided to have fun, to enjoy himself, and just go through the motions of playing football. Sometimes I was tempted to go through the motions, too.

When I got to Notre Dame in 1974, I knew it was going to be competitive. But I didn't know how competitive.

I discovered that there were seven quarterbacks in my freshman class—a couple of them were walk-ons, but at least one other, Gary Forystek, was, like me, a *Parade* All-American—plus the starter from the 1973 national championship team, Tom Clements, was back, and so was sophomore Rick Slager.

Ara Parseghian and his coaching staff decided that I would spend my freshman year on the scout team, pretending each week to be the quarterback on the next team we were going to face. The first-string defense spent each week pretending to hit me. Except they weren't pretending. They were brutal. Especially Mike Fanning and Greg Collins. They took turns beating up on me. Collins would knock me down and then ask me how I felt. "What's the matter, kid?" he'd say. "Did I hurt you?"

I did get to play in three junior varsity games, and even completed a pass. One pass, exactly. Three other quarterbacks, Forystek and two others, threw more passes than I did. I guess that made me the fourth-string quarterback on the junior varsity. Not quite a superstar.

I didn't get to know Parseghian well, but you could see that he was an easygoing and likeable guy who never acted like he was above anyone else. He had an uncanny ability to remember names. He'd meet your parents just once, and from then on, he'd always call them by their first names.

Parseghian was one of the reasons I'd decided to go to Notre Dame—my father's urging was the main reason—and when he resigned near the end of my freshman year, for personal and health reasons, I was sorry to see him go. He'd won two national championships in his eleven seasons at Notre Dame, and his teams had ranked among the top fifteen in the country every single season.

But my feelings were mixed. At least with a new head coach coming in—Dan Devine, who had been coaching the Green Bay Packers—we figured we were all starting fresh, we all had a chance to break into the lineup. I played well in the spring game, but when the fall came around, and the opening of the season, Devine decided that Rick Slager was going to be the starting quarterback. I was going to be on the bench.

Joe Montana sat on the bench the first two games of his sophomore season. Then, in the first period of the third game, against Northwestern, Slager got hurt, and Montana went in. Notre Dame was trailing, 7-0. Montana passed for one touchdown, ran for another and guided his team to a 31-7 victory. He was on his way—back to the bench against Michigan State the following week.

Then, against North Carolina, Montana got another chance. With his team losing, 14-6, in the fourth quarter, and Slager struggling, Devine called upon Joe. The Irish promptly drove seventy-three yards for a touchdown, and when Montana passed for a two-point conversion, the score was tied. With barely a minute left in the game, Joe threw a short pass to Ted Burgmeier, who turned it into an eighty-yard touchdown play. Notre Dame won. Montana was 2-0 as a reliever.

"[The Air Force game] was the first indication that he had the ability to be a great quarterback."
KEN MacAFEE, TEAMMATE, NOTRE DAME

He ran his record to 3-0 against the Air Force Academy. When Montana entered the game with thirteen minutes to play, Air Force was leading, 30-10, the game apparently won. But once again Joe soared in the final quarter. He led the Irish to three quick touchdowns. He ran for one of them and passed for another and beat Air Force, 31-30.

For the third time in four weeks, Montana had entered a game with Notre Dame losing, and he had wound up winning.

He was showing early signs of a special gift.

For the next two weeks, I was Devine's starting quarterback. But I played poorly when Southern Cal beat us, and then I broke my finger against Navy, and suddenly, my season was over. I had to go back to being a student.

It wasn't easy being both an athlete and a student at Notre Dame.

You'd wake up at seven-thirty in the morning, and the wind-chill factor was minus-thirty-five, and you didn't want to get out of bed, but you knew you had to. Otherwise, you'd get one of those notes from the academic advisor's office that says: "Please report to Mr. DeCicco's office immediately. No excuses will be accepted." And you knew right away that you were in trouble.

I just didn't see any purpose to studying accounting. I didn't think I'd ever need to know the difference between a debit and a credit. It was sort of like diagramming a sentence in English class. I suppose there's some reason for it, some method to the madness, but you sit there thinking, "Now why am I drawing these lines? Will I ever have to do this in my lifetime?"

NOTRE DAME 31

NORTHWESTERN 7

NOTRE DAME 21

NORTH CAROLINA 14

NOTRE DAME 31

PURDUE 24

Game ball from one of Montana's seven come-from-behind Notre Dame victories.

NOTRE DAME 21

CLEMSON 17

NOTRE DAME 26

PITTSBURGH 17

NOTRE DAME 35

HOUSTON 34

The accounting professor knew I didn't like the subject, and every time I walked into class, I'd be the first one he called on. I never was ready. I flunked accounting, the only course I ever flunked, and I had to make it up in summer school to stay eligible for football.

I spent just about all my summers in South Bend during my college years. One summer, I was a cook in a restaurant, serving up steak and lobster. Another summer, I worked for the parks department, dragging baseball fields and liming the baselines. And one year, I worked for a company doing market research. I took courses most summers, once because I had to—the accounting class—and the rest of the time because it made my schedule easier during the football season.

At the end of our last scrimmage before our first game in 1976, which was supposed to be my junior year, we were practicing short-yardage plays, trying to score from inside the ten-yard line. We ran plays over and over and, finally, Coach Devine told us to do it one more time, a play-action pass from the ten. I faked the handoff to the halfback, then turned to roll out and slipped. As I started to fall, I saw Willie Fry coming at me, 240 pounds of him, aiming straight for me. I knew he was going to hit me hard, but I didn't think it would be anything special, just another sack, another pounding. But Fry landed on top of me and pressed

"Just a regular guy who wanted to play hoops, go drink a beer. We called him Joe Montanalow because he was the spitting image of Barry Manilow."
DAVE HUFFMAN, TEAMMATE, NOTRE DAME

me into the ground, jolting my right arm, separating my throwing shoulder. For the second year in a row my season was ended by an injury.

I thought my football career might be over, too. I'd never hurt my throwing arm before. I didn't know what it would be like when it healed, and even if it healed perfectly, I couldn't be too cocky about the future. I was twenty years old, and after three years in college, I had completed a total of twenty-eight passes in varsity games. Twenty-eight passes in three years. There were guys who threw more completions in one game. If anyone had predicted that I'd play in the NFL someday, he would've been laughed at. I knew I wanted to play for Notre Dame, but I wasn't sure I was going to be able to. The thought of giving up football at that stage was a little frightening. It would have been like changing majors.

In the spring of 1977, I reached the peak of my game—my basketball game. I was part of the team that won the Bookstore Tournament, a month-long outdoor competition with no substitutions that, in those days, was open even to varsity players. The team we beat for the championship included Kelly Tripucka, who went on to play ten years in the NBA. Kelly once said that I could've been a pretty good college player, but I probably never would've made it to the NBA. I suppose he's right, but I don't know. If I had put more time into basketball…

"Well, I knew he was going to be good, but I never knew he'd be that good. The thing is, I don't think the guy ever feels pressure. The people around him feel it more than he does. I don't think he knows what it is. To him it's just football."

In the fall, I almost had a chance to find out. I almost gave up on football. I started the season playing third-string quarterback. Rusty Lisch was the starter, and Forystek was behind him. I didn't play in the opening game against Pitt; we beat the defending national champions. I didn't play in the next game, either; we lost to Mississippi.

At that point, Coach Devine and I had the kind of relationship you would expect between a player who thought he should be playing and a coach who thought he shouldn't be. An antagonistic relationship. I probably should've talked to him about it, but I never did. Not then. We've had dinner a few times since I left Notre Dame, and I understand him better now. I understand the difficulty of the position he was in.

In the third game of the season, we played Purdue, and Lisch started, and when we fell behind, coach Devine put Forystek in for him. Then Gary suffered a terrible injury, a broken collarbone, and I figured it would be my turn. But Devine went back to Lisch. I was furious. I stood on the sidelines and swore. If Forystek was hurt and Lisch wasn't playing well and Devine still wasn't going to use me, what sense was there in trying? So what if I was going to be back the next year. Lisch would be back, too, and Forystek, and

Devine, and that didn't seem to leave any room for me. I was about ready to give up.

But, finally, Devine gave me my chance. We were losing, 24-14, when I went in. Then in the fourth quarter, after we picked up a field goal, I passed to Ken MacAfee for one touchdown, and in the closing minutes we drove seventy yards for another touchdown that lifted us to a 31-24 victory.

I started the next game, and the next, and the next, every game that season, every game the next season, twenty-one starts in a row. We didn't lose another game in 1977. We won with our running and with our passing and with psychology. For the game against Southern Cal, Coach Devine surprised us by putting brand-new jerseys in our lockers just before the kick-off. Instead of our standard blue and gold jerseys he gave us green ones. Notre Dame had worn green during some of its greatest seasons, but never since 1963. The impact sent us out on the field sky-high. We beat USC by thirty points. Then we beat Navy by more, and Georgia Tech by more than that, and then I scored two touchdowns in the fourth quarter when we came from behind to beat Clemson, which had Steve Fuller at quarterback and Dwight Clark at end. We moved into the Cotton Bowl, to face the country's number one team, the University of Texas Longhorns.

"I remember Joe driving us down the field to win it in the fourth quarter, and I remember him having something like a second-and-fifty-two at one point and getting a first down out of it. But best of all I remember him taking off down the sidelines with two linebackers closing in on him, and I was yelling, 'Go out of bounds, Joe! Go out of bounds!' And there was this tremendous collision, and they went down in a heap and only one guy got up, and it was Joe."

DAN DEVINE, COACH, NOTRE DAME

Undefeated Texas, with Heisman Trophy-winner Earl Campbell and Outland Trophy-winner Brad Shearer, was favored to add the national championship trophy to its collection. But our defense did a terrific job of stopping Campbell, holding him to harmless gains, and our running attack was so effective that we won easily, 38-10, even though I had a pretty mediocre game. More important, the victory gave us the national championship.

In my final year, 1978, we lost our first two games, then won eight in a row, including a 26-17 victory over Pittsburgh. They were ahead, 17-7, in the fourth quarter, but then I completed seven passes in a row, two of them for touchdowns.

We faced Southern Cal in our final regular-season game, and once again we were losing in the fourth quarter, 24-6. We came back and took the lead, 25-24, but we made a mistake. We left them too much time. USC won on a last-second field goal, 27-25. I had the best game of my college career in the second half against USC. I completed more passes in that half than I ever had in a full game—seventeen. After the season I was voted an honorable mention All-American for the second year in a row.

In December, I graduated with a degree in business and marketing, but I still had one more college football game to play, in the Cotton Bowl against Houston. It was not a beautiful day in Dallas. The temperature dipped down to twenty degrees, and the wind whipped up to thirty miles an hour. The groundskeepers had to scrape an inch of ice off the artificial turf before the game. I'd been suffering from the flu most of the week, and by halftime, I felt much worse. We had wasted a 12-0 lead. We were behind by 20-12, and I was sick. I was shaking uncontrollably, my body temperature down to ninety-six degrees. I felt like I was sitting in a bucket of ice. The training staff poured me gallons of chicken soup, trying to warm me up from the inside out, and they covered me with blankets. I still kept shivering.

I sat out almost the whole third quarter, and we fell further behind, 34-12. I didn't want to end my college career on the bench. I wanted to get back in the game, if it was humanly possible. The chicken soup and the blankets worked. My temperature came back up to a normal 98.6 and when the doctors said it was okay for me to play again, Dan Devine put me back in the game. He knew it was my last

"I am affected by things, but I don't show it.
I'm emotional, but nobody knows it. At Notre Dame
I was awed by the place in general and lonely at
being away from home for the first time." JOE MONTANA

year, my last college game, and he knew how much I wanted to play. But if something didn't happen quickly, I knew he was going to take me out again.

With eight minutes left in the fourth quarter, we were still twenty-two points behind. Then we scored on a blocked punt, I passed for a two-point conversion, and we were fourteen points behind. Three minutes later, I ran for a touchdown and passed for another two points. Now we were six points behind.

But with less than two minutes to go, I fumbled, and Houston recovered. To most people our chances looked slim. With half a minute to go, Houston went for a first down on fourth-and-one in its own territory, and came up short. We got the ball on the twenty-nine-yard line, and moved down to the eight-yard line with six seconds to go.

Coach Devine called for a pass to Kris Haines, cutting toward the right side of the end zone. I was supposed to throw the ball low and away; he was supposed to make a diving catch. I threw the ball too low; Kris couldn't get to it. The clock stopped. Two seconds to play.

"Can you beat 'em again?" I asked Kris. He said, "Yes," and I smiled, and when Coach Devine asked me what I thought we should do on the final play of the game, I said, "Same play." I ran back to the huddle and told Kris, "Let's do it."

We did. Kris cut toward the right, just across the goal line. I rolled to my right. Time ran out. And then I threw the ball, low and away, and Kris dove for it. This time he reached it and held it and hit the ground and tumbled out of the end zone. The score was tied, 34-34.

Our regular placekicker, Chuck Male, had pulled a leg muscle and couldn't play, but his back-up, Joe Unis, who was from Dallas, came out and kicked the decisive extra point, but we were penalized for illegal motion. Unis had to kick it again, and he did, and my college career came to an end the way it had started. With a comeback victory, twenty-three points in seven and a half minutes.

"These players have done it for four years," said Coach Devine after the game. "It's amazing the number of comebacks they've had in winning games."

I didn't have much to say after the game. I was in no shape to talk. Or walk. I was so bruised, so cut up I was a scab from elbow to elbow, from knee to knee—they literally had to cut my pants off.

By the time I got back to the hotel, after the trainers and the doctors got through with me, all my teammates had gone out, and I had no idea where they were. So I sat in the hallway of the hotel, all alone with a case of beer, and celebrated the end of my college career.

"You have to have confidence not just in your own abilities,
but in those of the people around you."

JOE MONTANA

Golden years: The first of many helmets Montana wore to glory throughout his career in San Francisco.

In the 1960s, the Green Bay Packers of Vince Lombardi and Paul Hornung and Willie Davis dominated professional football. The Packers won five NFL championships in seven seasons, a feat no team has ever matched.

In the early 1970s, the Miami Dolphins of Don Shula and Larry Csonka and Larry Little dominated professional football. The Dolphins, the first team to play in three straight Super Bowls, won two and, in 1972, became the only NFL team to go through a full season undefeated and untied.

In the mid and late 1970s, the Pittsburgh Steelers of Chuck Noll and Franco Harris and Jack Lambert dominated professional football. The Steelers played in four Super Bowls and became the first NFL team to win four Super Bowls.

In the 1980s, the San Francisco 49ers of Bill Walsh and Joe Montana and Ronnie Lott dominated professional football. Like the Steelers, the 49ers played in four Super Bowls and won all four.

If Walsh was the genius of the 49ers, and Lott the fury, Montana was, in every sense, the field general, leading and inspiring, thinking and executing, modest and magnificent. It would be unfair, and inaccurate, to say that Joe Montana was not affected by pressure. He was. Under pressure, he played better.

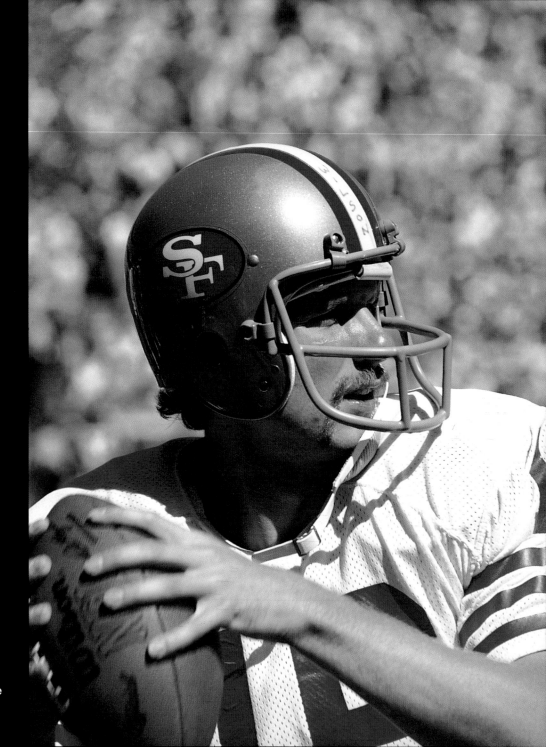

"I was sitting next to him at the counter in Howard Johnson's. Long blond hair, Fu Manchu mustache, skinny legs. I thought, 'This guy must be a kicker.' Then he introduced himself, and I couldn't believe this was the guy who brought Notre Dame back to beat us in the fourth quarter when I was at Clemson."

After I almost froze to death in the Cotton Bowl, I decided to move to Southern California, to live with one of my cousins in a three-bedroom apartment right above a bar called Joe's. The apartment was in Manhattan Beach, not far from the Los Angeles Airport. I'd had enough winters in Pennsylvania, Indiana, and Dallas. I wanted to thaw out.

I figured that any pro football team interested in me would have no trouble finding me. The Los Angeles Rams and the Green Bay Packers had me work out for them at a football field near the airport. The New York Giants flew me to New York for a tryout. Then the San Francisco 49ers came to Los Angeles to look at me.

Actually, they wanted to look at James Owens, mostly, a running back from UCLA. Owens was also a track man, a sprinter, and they wanted to see whether he might be the deep threat they were looking for. Bill Walsh, the new head coach of the 49ers, came in for the workout, along with Sam Wyche, his quarterback coach, and they had me throwing all kinds of passes to Owens—long, short, hard, soft, checking his speed, his hands, his athleticism. They seemed to be impressed by Owens, and by me.

The 49ers told me they were definitely interested, and so did a few other teams. On the day of the NFL draft, I went with my agent, a fellow named Larry Muno, whose son had been a punter with me at Notre Dame, to The Kettle, a restaurant in Manhattan Beach, and waited to see when I would be selected. The draft wasn't the big deal then that it is now. It wasn't televised, so Larry called his office every ten minutes or so to see if there was any word.

Three quarterbacks were selected in the first round, but I wasn't one of them. The Cincinnati Bengals chose Jack Thompson, the New York Giants decided to go for Phil Simms, and the Kansas City Chiefs took Steve Fuller.

I got a little nervous. "What am I going to do if I'm not picked?" I asked Larry, and he said, "Don't worry, you'll go."

I would've liked to have been picked in the first round, purely for selfish reasons. The higher you're drafted, generally speaking, the more money you get. But San Francisco didn't have a first-round pick—they'd traded it away—and in the second round, they selected James Owens.

The 49ers took me in the third round. I was the fourth quarterback drafted, the eighty-second player overall. Honestly, my feelings weren't hurt. Sure, I had some anxious moments, but I was just happy to be drafted. I had no idea what kind of a career I was going to have in the NFL— I don't think anybody else did either, not even Bill Walsh. I just wanted it to last as long as possible.

Just before training camp began, I signed, not for any huge amount, but enough to make me happy. Then I had to make the team. I knew the odds were in my favor. The 49ers had gone 2-14 in 1978, and they had been the lowest-scoring team in pro football. Steve DeBerg, their starting quarterback, and his back-up, Scott Bull, were both coming off tough seasons and knee surgery. But, as the start of the season approached, you saw guys getting released who you thought would make it, and you began wondering about yourself. When the final cut came, and my roommate Dwight Clark, then an unknown from Clemson, and I both survived, we were both relieved.

I was a rookie, my roommate was a rookie, and our head coach, Bill Walsh, was a rookie. He had just come in from Stanford and brought with him an assistant coach, Denny Green, who was put in charge of special teams. Green decided that I was going to be the holder for the place-kicker. Ever since then, every time I see Denny, who became head coach of the Minnesota Vikings, I tell him that I still hate him for that.

I'd never been a holder before. It's not just a bad job, it's the worst job in the world. Do it perfectly, nobody notices. Do it wrong, everybody notices. Our kicker my rookie year, and for most of my career in San Francisco, was Ray Wersching, and he was a very unusual kicker: he never blamed the holder when he missed. That made you work even harder to get everything right for him. We had another kicker trying out my rookie year who had a steel plate form-fitted into his kicking shoe. I hated to hold for him. I figured one slip, one bad kick on his part, and there goes my throwing hand.

"If you ever stopped to think about what happens, what really makes things tick, after the ball hits your hands, it might screw up the whole process."

JOE MONTANA

Looking back, I guess I'd say that I came into the National Football League in the best possible way. I didn't have to live up to any great hype, to anybody else's great expectations. I had an experienced quarterback in front of me, a tough, smart, talented football player, but not a big hero, not a monument. I was able to progress slowly, but surely. In 1979, I became a quarterback in the NFL. In 1980, I became a starting quarterback in the NFL. And in 1981, I became a winning quarterback in the NFL. I got a great deal of satisfaction out of each of those steps, especially the last one.

In 1979, Montana appeared in all sixteen 49er games, but usually just as a holder. He threw the first pass of his NFL career in the third game of the season, against the Los Angeles Rams.

Two months later, Montana threw his first NFL touchdown pass, his only one all season, against Denver, and two weeks after that, he made his first start, against St. Louis. He threw only twenty-three passes all season. Bill Walsh was trying to teach him and spare him at the same time.

Walsh didn't want me to take any unnecessary punishment, didn't want my confidence, or my body, to be shattered. He also wanted me to learn his system, which is complicated, far different from the system Dan Devine used at Notre Dame, far different from the systems most pro teams use. I tried to watch from the sidelines and figure out not only what was going on, but why it was going on, why this guy was here, why that guy was there, how it affected zones, how it affected man-to-man coverage. But sometimes you couldn't figure out what was going on, and you'd ask him.

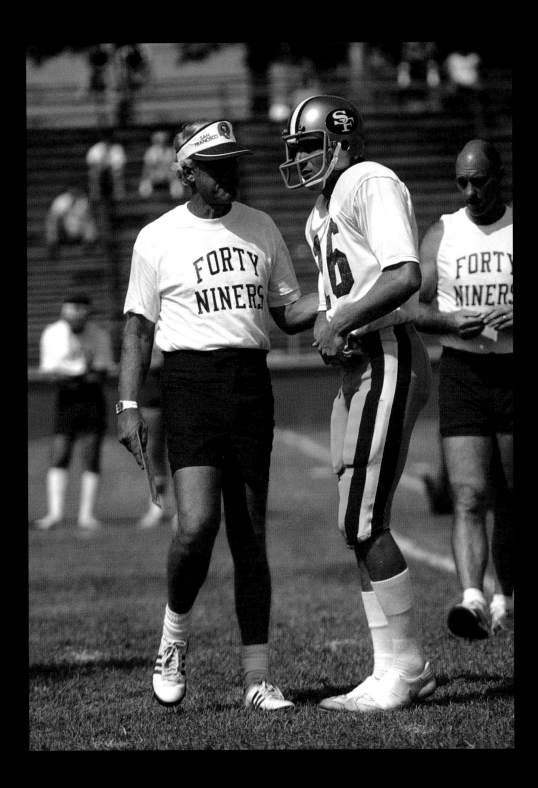

"Joe was the last quarterback we looked at. The minute I saw him drop back—his quick movement, those quick, nimble, Joe Namath-type feet—I got very serious."

BILL WALSH, HEAD COACH, 49ERS

"He can thread the needle, but usually goes with his primary receiver and forces the ball to him even when he's in a crowd. He's a gutty, gambling, cocky type. Doesn't have great tools but could eventually start." 1979 PRE-DRAFT NFL SCOUTING REPORT

Once and future heroes: (left to right) Dwight Clark, Joe Montana, Steve DeBerg.

Walsh is as smart as they come in football. His offense can attack almost any kind of defense. There are so many adjustments built into the offense that, in theory, no one should be able to stop you. It worked pretty well in practice as well as in theory.

Walsh's passing game is sort of like an upgraded running game. It's like a long handoff. Instead of handing the ball to a guy in the middle of the field, where he might have five or six guys trying to tackle him, you throw it to him off to the side and he only has to beat one man or maybe two. If he only gains four or five yards, that's okay. What you want is a constant attack; you want to keep moving down the field. And if it takes fifteen or sixteen plays to get a touchdown, all the better, because you're eating up the clock and keeping your defense off the field.

Memorization was the key to the whole system, and not just for the quarterbacks. Most teams would go into a game with maybe fifteen running plays and thirty passing plays, but we'd go in with thirty running plays and eighty or ninety passing plays, with two formations for most of the passing plays, three formations for some. When I called out the play in the huddle, the linemen had to know what their assignments were. You may not need to be a genius to play football, but you couldn't be stupid and play in that system.

I had to get to know my teammates, too. Four of the five offensive lineman who would be in front of me in our first Super Bowl were already with the 49ers when I arrived—Keith Fahnhorst, Randy Cross, Fred Quillan, and John Ayers. They were all in their twenties, starting to come together as a unit.

Quarterbacks always have a special feeling for their offensive line. These are guys who put you in the position to be able to do what you can do. Without them, there's no way you could accomplish anything. You respect them, and because they get so little recognition, you express your respect whenever you can. I made it a point to take every opportunity to say something to the media about my offensive line. The only trouble was the reporters got so tired of hearing about the line, they just quit printing what I said, and then the linemen would ask me, "How come you never say anything about us?"

Steve DeBerg knew I was competing for his job, but he couldn't have treated me better, couldn't have been more supportive. I admired him then; I admired him through his whole career, through seventeen seasons in the NFL. He started off as a tenth-round draft choice and had to battle for everything he achieved.

A couple of older veterans tried to make me comfortable, too: Cedrick Hardman, whose career with the 49ers had begun in 1970, and O. J. Simpson, who was finishing up his career with the team. Hardman was always a positive guy, always offering you advice and encouragement. He was the first guy I believed who told me that I'd make it in the NFL. "Someday you're gonna run this team," he said. "You'll get the chance. Hang in."

At the beginning of the 1980 season, Walsh still wasn't ready to make Montana his starting quarterback. He kept Joe on the sidelines till the third game of the season, against the New York Jets, and then he chose just the right spot to make Montana look good. Inside the Jets' ten-yard line, Walsh sent Montana in to run a bootleg. Joe rolled to his right and scampered, untouched, for the touchdown.

In the second quarter, Walsh let Montana throw, and he hit Dwight Clark for a touchdown. In the third quarter, Montana again passed to Clark for a touchdown, finishing off another drive DeBerg had started. It had to be frustrating for DeBerg, setting the plate for Montana, but the 49ers won their third game in a row, and, as Walsh had intended, Montana's confidence began to grow.

But the next week he was back on the bench, watching DeBerg play, watching the 49ers suffer the first of eight defeats in a row. The following week, after the 49ers fell far behind the Rams, Montana came off the bench and threw more passes, and completed more, than he had in his whole brief NFL career.

Then we played Dallas, and Walsh decided to protect me again. That day, the Cowboys killed us, and I just watched, I didn't play. I watched Steve take the hits from Randy White and Too Tall Jones and Harvey Martin. He got hit so hard I could feel it. For once in my life, I had no objection

"You couldn't lose sight of the fact that he was still a young player, and in game situations every play is almost crisis-like to a young player."

BILL WALSH
HEAD COACH, 49ERS

to staying on the sidelines. I stood behind Coach Walsh, and every time he turned around as if looking for someone to put in the game, I stepped away from his line of vision. If he turned to his left, I moved to his right and vice versa.

I started seven of the last ten games in 1980, the last five in a row, kicking off a string of forty-nine straight starts that didn't end until an injury in 1984.

We won three of those last five games in 1980, and one of those victories I still remember clearly. I don't live in the past, but I sure can recall the game against New Orleans in 1980.

The Saints had never had a winning season, but this was their worst. They had lost their first thirteen games. Their fans were calling them "The Ain'ts." And worse things. For some reason, they decided to take it out on us. Archie Manning was just unbelievable in the first half. He threw for three touchdowns, and at halftime, we were losing, 35-7. Walsh told us in the locker room he'd heard the Saints talking about winning the game maybe 70-7.

I don't know if that inspired us or not. I don't like losing by anything, one point or fifty, and I don't like giving up. I figured we still had to play the second half. And we did. We had two scoring drives in the third quarter and two more in the fourth. Each of them was more than 75 yards long. I ran for one touchdown, I passed for two, and we caught up at 35-35 in the closing minutes. Then Ray Wersching kicked a field goal in overtime; the Saints had their fourteenth consecutive defeat, and we had the greatest comeback victory in NFL history.

"**Most of the time a quarterback gets hit from about the last rib up, between there and the shoulder pads, and you're able to absorb the blow pretty well. But when you get sandwiched into the ground, when a guy pins you down, that's when it really hurts. And they are trying to hurt you.**" JOE MONTANA

New York Giants' linebacker Lawrence Taylor takes Montana down in the 1981 playoffs.

Montana and Clark celebrate another triumph.

Walsh traded Steve DeBerg to Denver before the start of the 1981 season. In a way, he did it for me, to let me know that I had come of age, that I was now his starting quarterback, but I think I was more upset than relieved. I really felt bad for Steve; we had become such good friends. But at least he was going to a playoff team that needed a quarterback.

We needed a stronger defense. For two years in a row, we had given up more than 400 points. In 1981, we drafted Ronnie Lott in the first round, Eric Wright in the second round, and Carlton Williamson in the third. All three became Pro Bowl defensive backs, Lott in his rookie season. We also picked up Dan Audick in 1981, the fifth member of our offensive line.

The 49ers struggled at the start of the 1981 season, losing two of their first three games. When they played the Dallas Cowboys, who had beaten them so badly the previous year, the 49ers were 3-2, the Cowboys 4-1. But San Francisco scored three touchdowns in the first quarter, coasted to an easy victory—and began to believe in themselves. With Montana at quarterback they won twelve of their last thirteen games, two of them coming from behind in the fourth quarter.

One of those comeback victories was in Pittsburgh, in front of people I had grown up with, against the Steelers, the team I had grown up idolizing. It was the first time I'd played in Pittsburgh—I'd played against Pitt in college, but that was in South Bend—and it was fun and exciting, but it was also nerve-wracking. Not only did I have to get a ton of tickets for friends and relatives, but I was in awe of playing guys I felt I'd been watching forever. Guys with names that I knew as well as my own, Terry Bradshaw and Franco Harris and John Stallworth and Lynn Swann and Mean Joe Greene—almost all the stars of the Steelers' four Super Bowl victories. I couldn't believe I was on the same field with them. We scored the winning touchdown in the fourth quarter, but it was our defense that won the game for us, forcing six turnovers, three interceptions, three fumbles.

San Francisco finished the regular season with a 13-3 record, the best in the NFL, the best in the 49ers' thirty-two years in the league. The first team they faced in the playoffs was the New York Giants, who had been a losing team for eight straight seasons.

Phil Simms, the Giants' quarterback for most of the season, was out with a separated shoulder, but his back-up, Scott Brunner, had a terrific game, passing for three touchdowns, keeping the Giants in contention till the fourth quarter. Then Ronnie Lott intercepted Brunner for the second time and returned the ball for a touchdown, clinching the victory, setting up The Catch.

"That's a strange world inside that circle out there. People are yelling and screaming almost like they want to see blood and guts ... So you have to have a different attitude in there."

JOE MONTANA

In Super Bowl XVI, the 49ers met the Cincinnati Bengals, whose recent history was strikingly similar to theirs. In 1979, the 49ers had the worst record in the NFC, the Bengals the worst in the AFC. In 1980, the 49ers improved slightly, to 6-10, and Cincinnati improved slightly, also to 6-10. They both became winners in 1981, and both wanted nothing more than to cap the season with a Super Bowl victory.

In the week before the game, I got my first exposure to the Super Bowl hype, to the daily press conferences attended by hordes of reporters. I don't know what was worse, listening to reporters asking the same questions over and over, or listening to me giving the same answers over and over. They were trying hard to get me to say something newsworthy, something that would stir things up, and I was trying hard not to. That part of it wasn't much fun for either side. Even though our press conferences began at 8:30 A.M. Eastern time—5:30 A.M. San Francisco time, I managed to stay awake, and I managed not to say anything exciting.

I was always wary of the media, or maybe wary of myself, wary of what I might say to the media. I would sort of put myself on automatic pilot when I faced reporters. There are lots of things you want to say, but you're afraid someone will take something out of context, and so you retreat into the predictable.

We played the Bengals in the Silverdome in Pontiac, Michigan, the first cold-weather site in Super Bowl history, but the weather was perfect inside the dome. So was the first half. Walsh, as usual, came up with a few special plays—he put in one of them just the day before the Super Bowl—

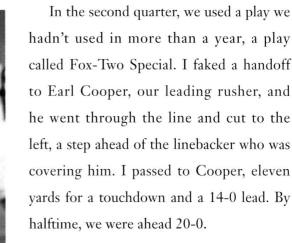

Despite the best efforts of a stubborn Cincinnati Bengals team, the 49ers prevailed in their Super Bowl debut appearance.

Facing page: *Montana joins his teammates on the field at the Pontiac Silverdome to face the Bengals in Super Bowl XVI.*

and on our first drive, we used a flea flicker, a trick play we had practiced many times. I handed off to Rickey Patton who handed off to Freddie Solomon who pitched the ball back to me, and I threw a pass to tight end Charle Young that gained fourteen yards and kept our drive alive. We ended up going sixty-eight yards for a 7-0 lead. I ran the final yard.

In the second quarter, we used a play we hadn't used in more than a year, a play called Fox-Two Special. I faked a handoff to Earl Cooper, our leading rusher, and he went through the line and cut to the left, a step ahead of the linebacker who was covering him. I passed to Cooper, eleven yards for a touchdown and a 14-0 lead. By halftime, we were ahead 20-0.

A reporter asked me afterward if it was nerve-wracking getting new plays the week before the Super Bowl, and I told him, "It happens all the time. We were afraid we were going to get a new play in the bus on our way to the game."

Our bus, carrying half the team, had gotten caught in a monster traffic jam before the game. We had to stand still and wait while Vice President George Bush's motorcade made its way to the stadium. We didn't move for about twenty minutes. Walsh was in our bus and he was pretty loose. "I've got the radio on," he told us, "and we're leading 7-0. The trainers are calling the plays."

Cincinnati fought back in the second half, cut our lead to 20-14, but in the final quarter we turned conservative, ran the ball most of the time, added two field goals and had a 26-14 cushion when the Bengals scored in the final minute of play.

We were the Super Bowl champions. I didn't have a spectacular game, but I was voted the Most Valuable Player. You always say that you have to share it with all your teammates, but this time everyone really did deserve a share. They all contributed, offense, defense, special teams, and, of course, the coaching staff.

Of all my years in pro football, that had to be one of the best. Winning something for the first time, particularly like we did, coming from the absolute bottom, changes the whole team, changes everyone's outlook. It gave us a bright outlook for the rest of our careers. You could almost say it made our careers.

But if 1981 was a high, the next season was a low, a season cut to nine games by a players' strike that I totally disagreed with. I'm not anti-union—you can't come from Western Pennsylvania, from United Steelworkers' and United Mine Workers' country and be anti-union—but I was against this strike. I disagreed with the leadership of the players' union, squabbled with Gene Upshaw, the president, and Ed Garvey, the executive director, and argued with their goals. I thought the strike was misguided and wasteful, that we should have been concentrating on free agency instead of a pay scale, but some of my teammates felt exactly the opposite. The unity that had helped make our team so successful in 1981 was replaced by antagonism.

Statistically, I had a pretty good season, but we finished the shortened season with three victories and six defeats. That was the last time I played on a team with a losing record.

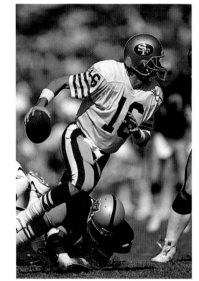

"He's a natural football player—really, a natural competitor. He competes instinctively. It's like he's so used to competing that he has no awe for it, nor for himself."
BILL WALSH
HEAD COACH, 49ERS

The next three years were good ones for Montana. He missed only two games, both against Philadelphia, one in 1984, one in 1985, both times with injuries to his sternum, his breastbone. The 49ers lost in the playoffs in 1983 and 1985, but in 1984, they enjoyed one of the greatest seasons in pro football history.

They won fifteen of sixteen games in the regular season—they were so strong they had to come from behind in the fourth quarter only twice all year— then three straight playoff games, each by more than ten points. In Super Bowl XIX, at Stanford Stadium, just down the peninsula from Candlestick Park, San Francisco beat Miami, 38-16. The 49ers sent ten players to the Pro Bowl, including the whole defensive backfield—Dwight Hicks, Ronnie Lott, Carlton Williamson, and Eric Wright. Four of the 49ers—Hicks, Montana, center Fred Quillan, and guard Randy Cross— were starters.

The Super Bowl was special, partly because we were playing so close to home, and partly because we were facing a great team with a great quarterback, Dan Marino. Marino had passed for more than 5,000 yards and for 48 touchdowns during the regular season, both NFL records that still stand. He had passed for more than 400 yards in four different games in 1984. That's unbelievable: I passed for more than 400 yards only seven games in my whole career.

The week leading up to the game, it seemed that all anybody talked about was Marino, how great he was, how he couldn't be stopped. Nobody seemed to be saying anything about our offense. We felt we deserved a little attention too.

"The guy is unflappable. There's nobody I've ever seen who is that calm and unperturbable. The guy can't be flustered in a big situation."
RANDY CROSS,
TEAMMATE, 49ERS

To complete their 1984 season, the 49ers squared off against the Miami Dolphins in Super Bowl XIX.

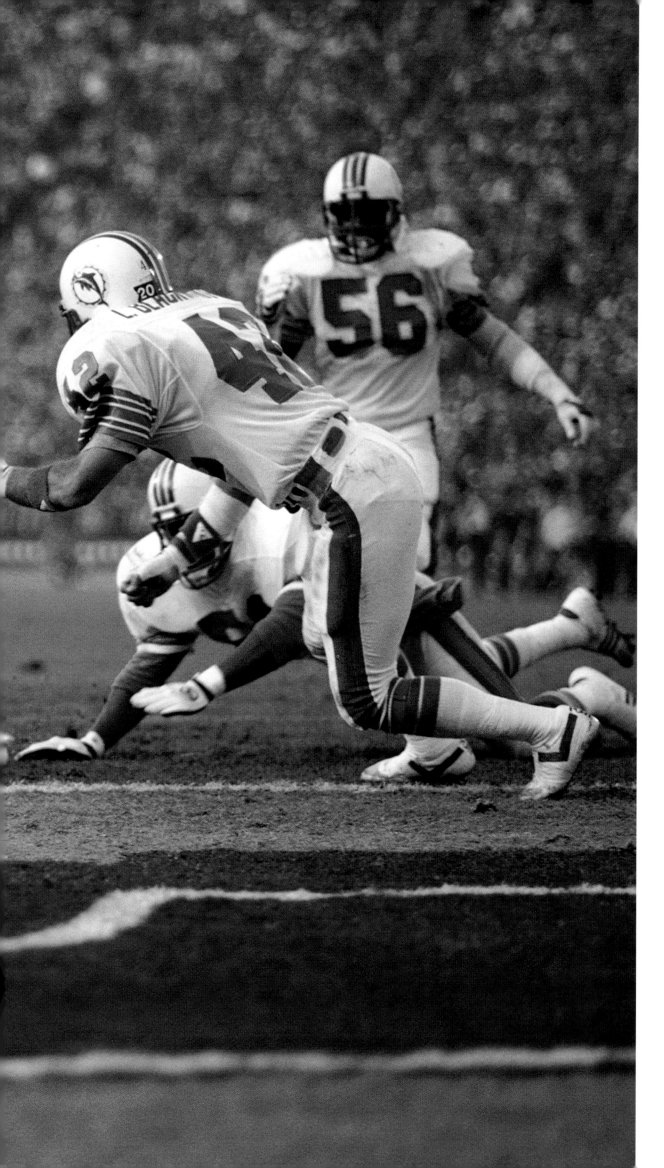

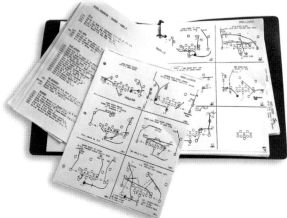

"Montana was outstanding in every way.
Every time we tried to put pressure on him,
he scrambled for a big play on his own or he
bought time to hit one of his receivers.
He hurt us in every way."

DON SHULA, HEAD COACH, MIAMI DOLPHINS

Above: *Montana's copy of the 49ers' playbook
for Super Bowl XIX.*

"We met during a Schick razor commercial, and my first impression of Joe was, 'Thank God, they got somebody tall enough.' The two men I had worked with before had to stand on apple crates. I'm six feet tall. Joe is six foot two." JENNIFER MONTANA

And they got it—in The New York Times: *"Joe Montana set a Super Bowl record with 331 passing yards and was voted the game's most valuable player ... Montana was, at times, a magician. He completed twenty-four of thirty-five passes, threw for three touchdowns and executed his plays magnificently."*

As far as I'm concerned, 1984 was a perfect year—and not just because of our success on the football field. I met my wife, Jennifer, in February 1984.

I was scared to death.

Not of Jennifer. Of doing a commercial with her. I'd done a few commercials before, but they were always by myself, and if I messed up, I could just do it over. But this time I was supposed to be a cowboy in a Schick razor commercial, and Jennifer—Jennifer Wallace was her maiden name—was playing the Schick sheriff.

We were in Los Angeles, and I guess she could tell how nervous I was by how much I was sweating. The director told her to try to get me to relax, so she pinched me on my butt. I got a big smile on my face, but I was still nervous. Having Jennifer standing there, so beautiful and so poised, didn't make me any calmer. It took us two days to shoot the commercial, and it wasn't till the end of the second day that I got up the nerve to ask her out for dinner. "I'm sure you're busy," I said, "but . . ."

To my amazement, she said she wasn't busy. We dated all through the off-season, and in August, the day after an exhibition game, I took her to a park in San Francisco and told her to look up at the sky. She almost didn't see the banner on the plane I had rented. It said "JEN WILL YOU MARRY ME? JOE."

To my amazement, Jennifer said yes. Our engagement lasted through the 1984 season—I don't think it was a coincidence that that was our best season—and we got married in 1985, after the Pro Bowl.

Marrying Jennifer would have been the highlight of any year. She made my life complete. She gave up a very successful career that she loved, to devote herself to me and to my career. I owe her so much. I don't know how I could have gotten through 1985 without her.

I started training camp with a lot of pain in my lower back, and even though the back responded to treatment and I was able to open the season, I certainly wasn't feeling one hundred per cent. We struggled in the early part of the year, losing four of our first seven games—everybody wants to beat the Super Bowl champion—and even though we managed to get into the playoffs as a wild-card team, we were knocked out in the first round by the New York Giants.

"Marrying Jennifer would have been the highlight of any year.
She made my life complete."

Our first child, Alexandra, was born during the 1985 season, and I admit, I was frightened, scared that I wouldn't be a good enough father. Of course I fell in love with Alexandra as soon as I saw her, and her presence took the sting out of practice sessions and out of defeat. When we were eliminated in the first round of the playoffs, it wasn't the end of the world. I had a wife and a daughter to go home to.

In 1986, we opened the season in Florida, against Tampa Bay. We won easily, and I had a big game, thirty-two for forty-six for 356 yards. But I threw one disastrous pass. I was running to my left, and I threw back to my right. No one hit me, but as I twisted my body to release the ball, I felt something snap. I didn't know what it was, and it didn't really hurt, not then, so I stayed in the game.

Afterward, I found out I had ruptured a disk. Or, as one doctor put my condition: "Congenital spinal stenosis (curvature of the spine) associated with an acute rupture of the L5-S1 disk." It sure sounded like I was in great shape.

I was going to need surgery.

Would I ever play football again? Nobody seemed to know for certain. Naturally, the possibility that I might not play again frightened me, but Jennifer and I were both more concerned with me having a normal life. After we sat and talked with the surgeon about the details of an operation, we both felt more at ease.

A week after the injury, I underwent a two-hour operation.

After the surgery, my left foot was numb. The doctor who operated on me said it might be permanent, but it wouldn't

"Joe functioned in a clear-headed manner, even in distress. He didn't lose it. It's like the soldier taking two in the belly and still finishing in charge."

BILL WALSH
HEAD COACH, 49ERS

affect my speed or strength. The doctor also said that I should be able to play football again in two or three months.

Six weeks later, the same doctor delivered a second opinion. He said that I was in excellent physical condition, that I was no more likely to be re-injured than I was before surgery, and that my recovery had been remarkably rapid. But he didn't think I should play football again.

"I don't recommend patients' going back to professional football after surgery," he said. "It's not a good idea. I wouldn't, and I wouldn't let my son."

I liked his first opinion better.

I had to learn to walk again after the operation. Jennifer and my therapist made sure I did. The therapist came to my house every morning, made me walk, made me exercise, no matter how much I complained. If I had had to go out to her clinic, I probably wouldn't have made it a lot of mornings. There were a lot of times when I didn't want to get up, when I wanted to just stay in bed. But she pushed me and so did Jennifer. Jennifer made me walk in the afternoons. She'd say, "*I* don't care if you don't play football again, but if *you* do, you're not going to get out of this." She made me feel guilty if I didn't work. I never worked so hard in my life. It was unbelievable.

On November 9, 1986, two months after my injury, after missing eight games, I returned to the starting lineup against the St. Louis Cardinals. I started the last seven games of the season, and we won five of them, finished first in our division, and met the New York Giants in the playoffs.

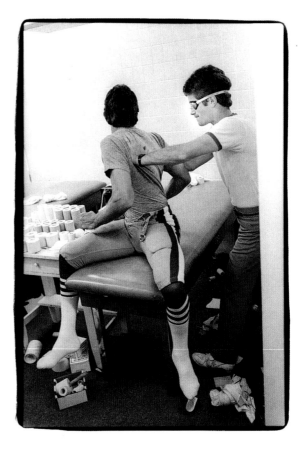

"No quarterback has ever been tougher, physically or mentally."

DAVE ANDERSON,
THE NEW YORK TIMES

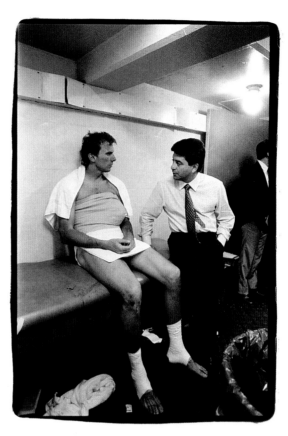

"He's like Lazarus. You roll back the stone, Joe limps out, throws off the bandages—and then throws for 300 yards."

TIM McKYER,
TEAMMATE, 49ERS

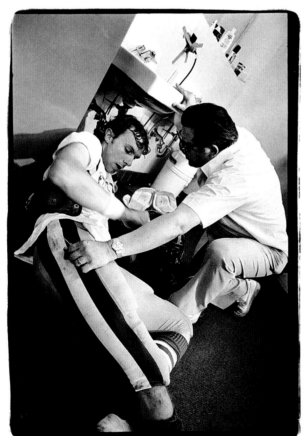

BROKEN FINGER

CRACKED RIBS

SEPARAT OULDER

A champion's suit of armor: (above) Montana's trusty shoulder pads,
worn throughout his pro career; (below) the "flak jacket" he often
used in an effort to protect his battered ribcage.

RUPTURED DISK

TORN ELB TENDON

BRUISED STERNUM

CONCUSSION

They killed us, and almost killed me. The record says they beat us 49-3, but I had no idea what the score was when the game ended. In the last minute of the first half, with the score 21-3, I dropped back and threw a pass toward Jerry Rice. As soon as I released the ball, Jim Burt, the Giants' nose tackle, smashed into me, full speed, straight into my ribs, driving me back, slamming me down. My head cracked against the hard artificial turf.

I never saw Lawrence Taylor intercept the pass and run it back for a touchdown. I just lay on the ground. I wasn't frightened because I didn't know what was going on. A lot of people watching were afraid that it might be my back, that I might've ruptured another disk or even been paralyzed. Jennifer was watching on TV, and she was frightened. Fortunately, Eddie DeBartolo, our owner, called her as soon as he found out that it wasn't my back, that I had suffered a concussion and was going to be all right.

Reigning monarch and heir apparent: Steve Young backed up Montana for four seasons as a 49er.

Facing page: *A punishing hit from Giants' nose tackle Jim Burt knocked Montana out cold and out of the 1986 playoffs.*

I was seeing double, had a miserable headache, and kept falling asleep. They gave me a brain scan and kept me overnight at a hospital in New York, but the next day I was ready to go home.

In April 1987, just before the NFL draft, the 49ers traded their second- and fourth-round choices to the Tampa Bay Bucs for their starting quarterback, Steve Young. I don't blame the 49ers. I don't blame Bill Walsh. Between my back and my head, and my age—I was about to turn thirty-one— the 49ers were smart to look for someone who might replace me. Some people were ready to write me off, but I wasn't ready to be replaced, not yet.

The 49ers had a good season in 1987, losing only two games, and late in the season, Montana completed twenty-two passes in a row, an NFL record. But the week after he set the mark, he hurt his left hamstring. He played only sparingly in the final three games of the regular season, and in the first playoff game, against Minnesota, he was ineffective. The 49ers lost, and Steve Young played the second half.

Young backed up Montana in 1987, 1988, and 1989, starting three games in each of those seasons while Joe coped with a series of minor injuries: After the hamstring, there was his back, an elbow, a knee, a rib, but nothing that kept him out for more than a week or two at a time.

Walsh tried to play mind games with both of us, sometimes indicating that Steve would be his starter even if I were healthy, sometimes suggesting that my career might last longer and the team might do better if I were the back-up.

I resented it at the time. I thought I had earned Walsh's respect, that I deserved it, and I couldn't understand why, in my mind, he wasn't giving it to me. We had always had differences— he sometimes seemed to be saying that his system was so good any quarterback could make it work, a theory I didn't necessarily agree with—but, at the same time, we had always had respect for each other. I knew how smart he was. I knew how smart his assistants were. I knew how much I gained from working directly with the quarterback coaches, with Sam Wyche, Paul Hackett, and Mike Holmgren, in that order. I knew Walsh did the thinking, the planning, the dreaming, and we executed—we turned his thoughts into actions.

One of the good things about Bill was that you could talk to him, you could tell him you disagreed with him, but I didn't do that as often as I should have. When he favored Young over me, it probably would've been the best thing to talk to Walsh, but I didn't. I was hurt, but I realize now that he had no choice, he had to build up Steve, the way he had built me up in my early seasons. He had to get Steve ready for the day when injuries or age would slow me down. It's hard to be friends with a head coach—the nature of the relationship doesn't really permit it—but once Bill stepped down as head coach, we became friends. The barriers to being honest with each other came down.

We won back-to-back Super Bowls in 1988 and 1989. You can't do much better than that. In 1988, it wasn't easy, not at the beginning, not at the end. We lost five of our first eleven games, and only a strong finish got us into the playoffs. If New Orleans had beaten us in the next-to-last game of the regular season, the Saints would have gone to the playoffs, and we would have stayed home.

We peaked at just the right time. We beat Minnesota and Chicago in the playoffs, by more than three touchdowns each, and then went to Miami, to face Cincinnati once again in a Super Bowl. We fell behind, 6-3. We fell behind, 13-6. And late in the fourth quarter, we fell behind, 16-13. Then we got the ball on our own eight-yard line with three minutes and ten seconds left in the game.

"It didn't matter whether it was a Monday night or it was a Super Bowl, there was enough pressure there and you'd just try to help everyone get through it."
JOE MONTANA

In the huddle, some of the guys seemed tense and nervous, especially Harris Barton, a great offensive tackle who had a tendency to get uptight. I wanted to figure out a way to get Harris to relax and just then I spotted John Candy, the actor, in the stands. He happened to be in my line of vision. "Look, isn't that John Candy?" I said, and everybody kind of smiled, and Harris relaxed, and then we could all concentrate on the game and on going ninety-two yards for a touchdown. We could all concentrate on The Drive.

We started moving, and I was calling two plays at once, trying to save time. We got as far as the Cincinnati thirty-five, and then a penalty pushed us back to the forty-five, second down and twenty to go. The next play, Jerry Rice managed to catch a pass in the middle of three Cincinnati defenders, broke loose from them, and took the ball all the way down to the eighteen-yard line, first down and ten to go. A pass to Roger Craig brought us to the ten-yard line.

The next play was 20 Halfback Curl X-Up. Jerry went in motion to the left and cut to the left flat, the decoy on the play. Craig started on the right and cut into the middle. He was the primary receiver, but he got slowed up. John Taylor, on the left side, ran straight down the seam and into the end zone. He was in full stride when he caught the pass for the touchdown that gave us our third Super Bowl championship.

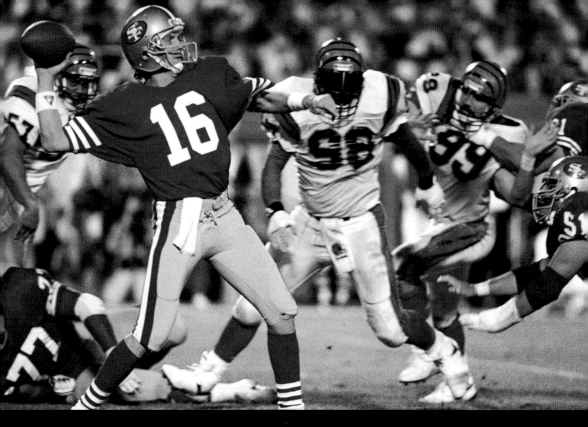

A future Hall-of-Famer in action. The Drive and the victory: Super Bowl XXIII vs. Cincinnati Bengals.

*Airborne high-five: Montana celebrates
with long-time teammate Guy McIntyre
during 49ers' 55-10 triumph over Denver
Broncos in Super Bowl XXIV.*

Montana with Jerry Rice, his all-time favorite touchdown receiver.
As 49er teammates they combined for fifty-five TDs in regular-season play.

Jerry Rice was named Most Valuable Player, and he certainly deserved it. Of the twenty-three passes I completed, Jerry caught eleven of them for 215 yards, a Super Bowl record.

Even my mother got interviewed after the game. She was quoted in *Sports Illustrated*:

"When they started the last drive, do you know what I was thinking?… The 1979 Cotton Bowl, when he brought Notre Dame from behind in the fourth quarter. That was the best—until now."

In 1989, Bill Walsh decided to step down, and in George Seifert's first season as head coach, the 49ers came almost as close to perfection as they did in 1984. They won seventeen games and lost two—by a total of five points. They lost to the Rams by one point, to Green Bay by four. They came from behind in the fourth quarter during four of their regular-season victories. They trailed Philadelphia by eleven points going into the fourth quarter, Los Angeles by fourteen, and won both those games.

We had to play one game in Stanford Stadium because of the damage done to Candlestick Park by the earthquake. I was at the park when the quake hit. Jennifer and I and our infant son, Nathaniel, had gone to see the World Series game between the Giants and the Oakland A's. We were just coming out of Eddie DeBartolo's suite right under a cement overhang, when everything started to tremble. I could see the light towers rocking back and forth. For a second we didn't know what it was—I'd never been in a big quake before. Then somebody said it was an earthquake, and the overhang started shaking. We thought it might come down on us, and we tried to get back inside. But the quake was over by then, and Jennifer and I began to worry about people stampeding out of the stadium. We were worried about the baby.

But it was weird. Hardly anybody left. People in the Bay Area were so used to earthquakes, they just sat down, they thought the game was going to go on. We had our two girls with our babysitter at her boyfriend's house, which wasn't too far from Candlestick. We couldn't get through to her, or to anybody else, so we made our way to the car. But traffic wasn't moving at all, so we sat in the parking lot for hours wondering and worrying. When we finally got the girls and the babysitter, they were fine, but it was scary.

During the 1989 regular season, Montana had a passing rating of 112.4, the highest in NFL history, and in the playoffs, he was even better. He completed seventy-eight per cent of his passes for 800 yards and eleven touchdowns—without a single interception. In Super Bowl XXIV, he threw five touchdown passes as the 49ers crushed Denver, 55-10, to win their fourth Super Bowl.

Montana was named Super Bowl MVP for an unprecedented third time, and he was named the regular-season MVP. Not bad for a guy whose career was supposed to be over almost four years earlier.

In 1990, when he was thirty-four years old, in his twelfth season with the 49ers, Montana threw more passes and gained more yards than he ever had before. He missed one game with a strained lower abdomen, but started every other game. Against Atlanta, he threw six touchdown passes and passed for 476 yards, both 49er records. Once again, he was the regular-season MVP, and Sports Illustrated *chose him as its Sportsman of the Year.*

The 49ers won their first ten games and went into the playoffs with a 14-2 record, the best in the NFL, beat the Redskins in the first round of the playoffs, then faced the New York Giants for the right to go back to the Super Bowl.

The Giants beat us, 15-13, and again they beat up on me. Leonard Marshall hit me harder than I'd ever been hit in my whole career. He hit me from the blind side, cracked a rib, bruised my sternum and then, as we were falling to the ground, he grabbed my hand, snapped it back and broke it. My chest hurt so bad I didn't even realize my hand was broken. We lost on the last play of the game—a forty-two-yard field goal. We came that close to a chance to win the Super Bowl for the third year in a row.

I didn't realize it at the time, but that was, basically, the end of my football career in San Francisco. In training camp in 1991, my right elbow was bothering me, and the trouble was diagnosed as tendinitis. In October, I had surgery to repair a torn tendon in the elbow. I was on injured reserve the rest of the year, didn't play a down, just stood on the sidelines and tried to give some good advice to Steve Young.

It's no secret that Steve and I were never close, that we weren't buddies, that we were on different wavelengths, but I've always respected him as a football player, especially

Sports Illustrated's *Grecian Amphora, awarded to* Joe Montana, *1990 "Sportsman of the Year."*

as a runner. And I wanted to see the 49ers win. I have too much respect for the organization, for Eddie DeBartolo in particular, not to want to see them win.

But I would rather have seen them winning with me healthy and in the lineup.

The next year, 1992, I had swelling in a muscle in my right elbow during training camp and again had to undergo surgery on the elbow. I sat out the first fifteen games of the season, most of them because I wasn't physically ready, some of them because George Seifert didn't want to disturb the chemistry of a winning team.

For any player, it's uncomfortable to stay on the sidelines. If you're comfortable there, you'll always be there. Standing there knowing you can play, and not being allowed to, is the worst situation. Your mind wanders. You wonder what you would have done—or how you would have done.

Finally, in the last game before the 1992 playoffs, I got a chance to play. Coach Seifert put me in for the second half against Detroit. Remember, I hadn't played in two full seasons. It was, in a way, the most difficult situation I ever faced on a football field.

I knew deep inside me that this was the last time I was going to play for the 49ers. I knew they weren't going to use me in the playoffs no matter what I did. I knew that if I wanted to be a starting quarterback again, it was going to have to be somewhere else. And to have that opportunity, I really had to perform against Detroit, I really had to prove myself again. I knew that if I didn't show I could still play, no one was going to take a chance on me.

What was going to happen with the rest of my career was probably going to be based on what happened in one half of one meaningless game. I knew that my teammates wanted

to play well for me, I knew they wanted to make me look good. But they had nothing at stake. They were going to the playoffs, anyway. They had clinched the home-field advantage for all their playoff games. They just didn't want anybody to get hurt.

I was happy with the way I played. I completed fifteen of twenty-one passes, two for touchdowns. I also ran with the ball three times and picked up a few yards. After the game, I asked for the two touchdown balls, which I almost never did, but these two I wanted to keep. I went around to my teammates and said goodbye. To Harris and Jerry and John, to guys who'd blocked for me, and guys who'd caught my passes, to defensive players, too, to thank them for all the great years. I told them I wouldn't be back the next year, and they didn't believe me. They didn't think, one, that I'd do it, or two, that the 49ers would let me do it. It was very, very hard for me to say goodbye. I didn't want to leave the 49ers, but I knew it was best for everyone, I knew it was my only chance.

I dressed for the playoffs, but Seifert never used me. Dallas beat us for the conference championship and went on to win the Super Bowl.

Soon after the Super Bowl, Seifert announced that, even if I was healthy, Steve Young was his starting quarterback. Steve had two terrific seasons in 1991 and 1992, but I hadn't done too badly either in my most recent seasons. I had had three of the best years anyone ever had, and we almost won three

After sitting out the first fifteen games of the 1992 season, Montana led his 49ers, one last time, to victory over the Detroit Lions.

Super Bowls in a row, which no one had ever done. All I wanted was a fair opportunity to compete for the starting job.

Seifert felt that a competition, Steve or Joe, Joe or Steve, would have been distracting, would have undermined Steve's confidence. I think it would have been more distracting to Seifert than to Steve. Seifert wanted to be his own man. He was the head coach now, not Walsh, and he wanted his own man at quarterback. He had his opinion, and I had mine, and, unfortunately, they weren't the same.

I had to move on, I had to go somewhere else.

The 49ers tried to keep me, but not very hard. The owner of the 49ers, Eddie DeBartolo, did try—he really tried. We had a very close friendship and I knew he didn't want to see me leave. But, he didn't like to interfere with football decisions— Eddie went to Notre Dame, but he knew he wasn't Rockne.

Eddie and I talked several times during this period. I flew to his home in Ohio. It was important to me that he understand why I had to leave. I told him it was all about being a competitor, and because he is such a competitor himself, I think he understood. He knew it was the best thing for me, and the best thing for his team.

I truly hated the thought of not finishing my career in San Francisco, but I had two young sons who had never seen me play football. I didn't want them to see me standing on the sidelines, talking on the phone.

I wanted them to see me play.

"The success of this organization, how we've been treated, how we travel, how much we make, it's a tribute to Joe, the guy who wears number 16."

HARRIS BARTON, TEAMMATE, 49ERS

Montana's game-worn uniform from his last game as a 49er.

II III IV V

VI VII VIII

IX X XI XII

XIII XIV XV

SAN FRANCISCO 49ERS 26 – CINCINNATI BENGALS 21

XVI XVIII

SAN FRANCISCO 49ERS 38 – MIAMI DOLPHINS 16

XIX XXI

SAN FRANCISCO 49ERS 20 – CINCINNATI BENGALS 16

XXII XXIII

SAN FRANCISCO 49ERS 55 – DENVER BRONCOS 10

XXIV XXV

XXVI XXVII

"San Francisco still will have the Golden Gate Bridge, cable cars, Fisherman's Wharf, North Beach, and the best marriage of city, sea, and sky in America, but it will no longer have Joe Montana."

TOM BROKAW, NBC NEWS

New colors: After more than a decade in 49er trim, Montana donned the red and white of the Kansas City Chiefs.

5

In the early years of the merger between the National Football League and the American Football League, few teams were so strong as the Kansas City Chiefs. They lost Super Bowl I, won Super Bowl IV, and enjoyed nine straight winning seasons, finishing either first or second in their division in eight of those years. Their leader was their quarterback, Len Dawson.

Then Dawson retired, and the Chiefs stumbled. They suffered through six straight losing seasons, only one winning season in twelve years. They went twenty-one years in a row without winning a post-season game, twenty-three years in a row without getting to the AFC Championship Game.

How could they regain their glory? How could the Chiefs become Super Bowl contenders again?

Simple: Sign Joe Montana.

The problem was, the Phoenix Cardinals also wanted Montana to play quarterback for them in 1993.

The Cardinals offered Montana substantially more money, enough to make him the highest-paid player in the NFL. But the Chiefs offered Montana a better opportunity.

An opportunity to get to the Super Bowl.

I visited both Kansas City and Phoenix, worked out for both teams, showed them that my elbow and my back were fine. When I was throwing in Phoenix, Gary Clark, the receiver they had just acquired from Washington, got down on his knees on the field and said, "See? I'm begging him to come here."

The Chiefs were very complimentary, too. I liked the owner, Lamar Hunt, and I liked the head coach, Marty Schottenheimer. They had been a winning team for four straight seasons under Schottenheimer, and their new offensive coordinator was Paul Hackett, who had been my quarterback coach in San Francisco for three years. He was going to put in the same offense we had used with the 49ers.

I picked Kansas City.

At first, the 49ers, who had told me they would not stand in the way of a trade, balked, demanding a better deal from the Chiefs. But, eventually, on April 20, 1993, with a little prodding from Mr. DeBartolo, the trade was made. The Chiefs gave up a first-round draft choice for me and David Whitmore.

I had no illusions. I was going to have to prove myself all over again. I'd had to prove myself at Notre Dame; what I'd done at Ringgold High didn't mean anything. I'd had to prove myself in San Francisco; what I'd done at Notre Dame didn't mean anything. And now what I'd done in San Francisco didn't mean anything in Kansas City.

It really hit me that I wasn't a 49er any more when I shot a commercial not long after the trade. They sent three Kansas City jerseys to my home: #3, the number I'd worn at Notre Dame; #16, the number I'd worn in San Francisco; and #19, the number I'd worn with the Monongahela Little Wildcats. The Chiefs had retired #16, Len Dawson's number, and even though Len offered to allow me to unretire it, I didn't think that was right. I chose #19, my Pop Warner number, and when I pulled on the red, gold, and white jersey of the Chiefs, I kept staring into the mirror, thinking I looked so strange. It had been so long since I had worn anything but 49er colors.

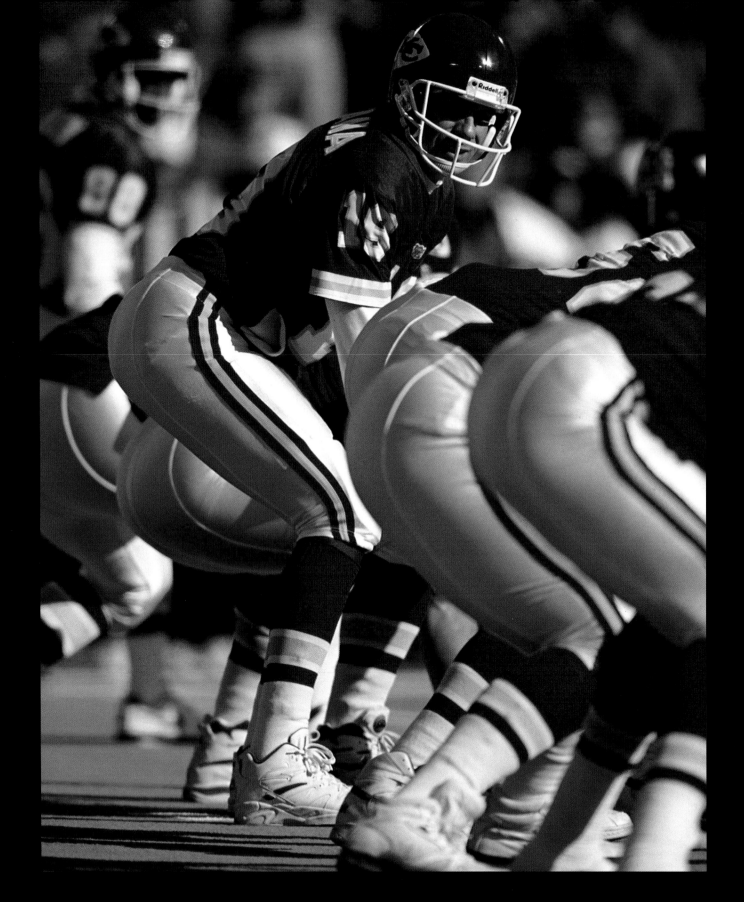

"A lot of guys, when it's fourth and whatever, they don't want to be in the play,
they don't want any part of it. He loved it. He thrived on it.
He wanted to be the guy who made the play."

MARCUS ALLEN, TEAMMATE, KANSAS CITY CHIEFS

In training camp, I found out that the Chiefs had some great players: Derrick Thomas and Neil Smith on defense, John Alt on the offensive line, Nick Lowery, the kicker, all coming off Pro Bowl seasons. The wide receivers Willie Davis and J. J. Birden were young and fast and looked like they would fit into the system. And there was another newcomer on the team, Marcus Allen, whose situation was a lot like mine. He'd spent his whole career with the Raiders, had set records for them and led them to a Super Bowl victory, and then he had been discarded. I didn't know Marcus well, but I'd known him a long time. We'd been rivals in college; he was a freshman at USC when I was a senior at Notre Dame. I knew Marcus could block, I knew he could catch passes, I knew how much he wanted to win. He felt he had to prove himself again, too.

I also found out that the Chiefs were my kind of guys. I had developed a reputation over the years as a practical joker. Why, I can't imagine.

When I arrived in Kansas City, I found my reputation had preceded me. The first or second day of practice, Bennie Thompson, a young defensive back, put shaving cream in my helmet. He thought I'd put the helmet on and get a headful of shaving cream. What did he think I was, a rookie? I looked in my helmet before I left the locker room, and as soon as I saw the shaving cream, I knew I was home.

We opened our season in Tampa Bay. I wouldn't even have remembered it was the same place I hurt my back in 1986 if other people hadn't brought it up. But I did know that the coach of Tampa Bay was Sam Wyche, who had

Two future Hall-of-Famers as Chiefs teammates: Montana with Marcus Allen. Previous pages: *A hero's welcome: Kansas City's faithful roar their approval as Montana sprints onto the field at Arrowhead Stadium for the first time as a Chief.*

scouted and coached me for the 49ers, and the starting quarterback for the Bucs was my old friend Steve DeBerg. Steve had been the starting quarterback in Kansas City for three or four years before I got there. Just in case I forgot that, I found a pair of size-fifteen football shoes in my locker at Tampa Bay, with a note from Steve: "Stop trying to follow in my footsteps."

In two years, Montana had played only one half of football, one half of a meaningless game. He celebrated his return by completing his first eight passes in a row. The Chiefs beat Tampa Bay, 27-3, and after his first game in the American conference, Montana was named the AFC Offensive Player of the Week.

It was a nice way to return, except that in the third quarter, I sprained my right wrist. It was dumb, my own fault. I threw to the wrong man. I should have thrown the short pass, but, instead, I tried to throw across the field, and as I released the ball, off-balance, I slipped. I stuck out my right hand to cushion the fall, but the hand was upside-down, and when it hit the ground, it bent the wrist and sprained it. Well, at least I didn't rupture a disk trying to throw across the field.

Right before the game, Jennifer had said to me, "Don't get hurt," and I'd said, "Oh, no!" Every time somebody tells me not to get hurt, I do.

The next week, we played Houston, and even though I wanted to play, even though it wasn't a major injury, Marty decided to protect me from the Oiler defense and the Astrodome turf. Dave Krieg, who'd become a good friend, took over as quarterback and took the beating: four sacks and two interceptions.

"If I put a game plan in, within twenty minutes Joe's got seventy per cent of it memorized. The next day, he's basically got it all. And he memorizes this stuff down to an amazing level. You can't shake him, even in a game."

PAUL HACKETT, OFFENSIVE COORDINATOR, KANSAS CITY CHIEFS

I was back the following week, and we beat Denver. (John Elway said to me before the game, "Stay healthy," but I still managed to get through it with nothing worse than a bruised chest.) And then we played the Raiders. A couple of days before the game, I was pulling out of the parking lot at Arrowhead Stadium, and Marty happened to be leaving at the same time. He waved, pulled up next to me, rolled down his window, and said: "Remember the new rule. You know you can throw the ball away. If you're out of the pocket, throw the ball away." I said, "Sure."

But you get in a game, and your instincts take over. In the second quarter, against the Raiders, I came out of the pocket and I saw the guy covering Marcus Allen turn his back and I knew I could pick up four or five yards, so I started running. Who would have thought I'd pull a hamstring?

I don't know whether I pulled the muscle myself, running, or if it happened when the guy from the Raiders rolled into me out of bounds. It didn't make much difference.

The hamstring really hurt, and in the locker room after the game, Marty said to me, "Remember what I said about the new rule. You can throw the ball away."

I told him I'd try to remember.

A sprained wrist, a strained hamstring, not serious injuries, not the kind that can keep you out for long. Just long enough to make people say, "Look how brittle he is; we told you he couldn't make it through the season."

You hate to listen to all that.

Some people tried to console me by saying it's a long season. I kept thinking, yeah, but it's getting shorter. I just wanted to play.

Montana sat out the following week, returned against San Diego and guided his team to a comeback victory. With less than three minutes to play and the Chargers leading, on fourth and ten, Montana hit Willie Davis for twelve yards. Marcus Allen then ran for the touchdown that gave the Chiefs a 17-14 victory, and Montana was again voted AFC Offensive Player of the Week.

Against Miami, Montana strained his hamstring again, worse this time, and sat out the next three games. Ten games into the season, the Chiefs were 7-3, and Montana had already missed half of the games.

I don't know whether the pain was worse mentally or physically. Jen told me the one thing she remembered from when I was playing all the time was how sore I always used to be. I guess I'd forgotten.

"I think that Montana in San Francisco was, to som
extent, beneficiary of the offensive system and the
players around him. But make no mistake: Joe Mon
was the reason the 49ers won four Super Bowls."

MARTY SCHOTTENHEIMER, COACH, KANSAS CITY CHIEFS

Standing in the pocket during a game: "If you've ever gotten stuck in the median, and it's not very wide, and you feel the cars whizzing by, and you know if you move in one direction or the other you'll get hit—that's about the same thing." JOE MONTANA

Montana didn't miss another game. He played the last six games of the regular season, and the three playoff games. His first game back, the Chiefs beat Buffalo, the defending AFC champions, and Joe was the conference Offensive Player of the Week for the third time in the six games that he'd played. A few weeks later, he suffered a mild concussion against San Diego, but had to leave the game only briefly. The Chiefs ended up 11-5 for the season and won the Western Division championship.

In the opening round of the playoffs, Kansas City faced the Pittsburgh Steelers, and it was so cold at Arrowhead Stadium, Montana started the game wearing gloves. His first seven passes went incomplete, and he discarded the gloves.

His ribs got banged up in the first quarter, and Dave Krieg came in, threw one pass, and connected for a touchdown. Still the Chiefs were losing 24-17, till, on fourth down with less than two minutes to play, Montana passed to Tim Barnett for a touchdown. Nick Lowery missed a field-goal attempt that would have won the game in regulation, but he didn't miss in overtime.

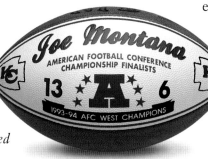

The Chiefs, led by Montana, won thirteen of nineteen games they played in 1993, and reached the AFC Championship Game for the first time in two decades.

Kansas City advanced to the next round against Houston. The Oilers had won eleven straight games, and took a 10-0 lead in the first quarter. It was still 10-7 going into the fourth quarter, but the Chiefs scored three touchdowns in the last nine minutes—Montana threw two touchdown passes less than a minute apart—and moved into the AFC Championship Game, against Buffalo in Buffalo.

On that same day, the NFC Championship Game was being played in Dallas, the Cowboys against San Francisco. If we could win, and if the 49ers could win, we would meet in the Super Bowl. I tried not to even think about it.

We both got beat, the Chiefs and the 49ers. Buffalo had us 20-6 at the half, and on the third play of the third quarter, I got hit in the head so hard it felt like a lightning bolt went right through my helmet. Another concussion. I didn't play again. Krieg did a great job coming off the bench, but we couldn't catch up to the Bills.

As soon as my head was clear, I started thinking about retirement. I didn't know how many more concussions I could take. The people who hit me were getting bigger and stronger and faster every year.

It was nice that I was selected for the Pro Bowl for the eighth time (I was in no shape to play in it), but it was even nicer that Marcus Allen was selected. During the regular season, Marcus ran for more than 700 yards and scored twelve touchdowns, his busiest and best season in five years. He gained more than 100 yards and scored two of his touchdowns against the Raiders, and, even better, we beat the Raiders twice. Marcus never said a word about wanting to do well against his old team, never verbalized his feelings, but I probably knew better than anybody how much those games meant to Marcus.

A few weeks after the season, the memories of concussions and contusions began to fade, and so did the idea of retirement. I thought about it, and football was still fun, still a challenge. And I still had dreams about a fifth Super Bowl. We didn't exactly miss by much in 1993.

Besides, in 1994, Nicholas, my youngest child, turned two, and he could come to the locker room along with Nathaniel, his four-year-old big brother. Nathaniel loved coming in after the games. He called my locker my "closet."

"We got so close last year, my reaction was, let's give it another shot. We're all here for one reason and that's to get to the Super Bowl." JOE MONTANA

Kansas City was a good place to live, and a good place to play football. We had a nice home, good neighbors, and fantastic fans who lived and died with the Chiefs. I would have loved to have won a championship for them and for the owner, Lamar Hunt.

We started the 1994 season with three straight victories, including, in the second game, a victory over San Francisco. The game was built up almost like a Super Bowl—Joe against Steve again, Joe against his former teammates— but I tried to think of it as just another game. "Joe never mentioned to us what this game meant to him," Neil Smith told reporters after the game, "and what it was all about. But we knew that deep down inside he really wanted it. And so did we."

Deep down inside, of course, I wanted to win every game.

Steve Young and I wished each other luck before the game, and exchanged compliments after the game, just a few words. We do have respect for each other; we just don't have a whole lot of warmth.

The second-largest crowd in Kansas City history jammed Arrowhead Stadium for the confrontation, and the Chiefs took a 7-0 lead in the first quarter when Montana threw a touchdown pass to an offensive lineman, Joe Valerio, who had lined up as an eligible pass receiver.

Young brought the 49ers back in the second period and led at the half, 14-9. Then, in the third quarter, Montana passed for one touchdown, Marcus Allen ran for another, and the Chiefs went on to win, 24-17. Turnovers were the difference: The Chiefs had none; Young fumbled twice and threw two interceptions. Young was also sacked four times.

Certainly, I felt good about winning, about beating my former team, but I didn't gloat, I didn't feel like I'd taken revenge on them. I still had too many friends on that team. I was still rooting for them to get to the Super Bowl—and find us there.

But not the way we played in our fourth and fifth games. We not only lost both games, we didn't score a touchdown. Not a touchdown in two weeks. The Rams shut us out, the first shutout of my career, and the Chargers held us to a couple of field goals.

For the first time in my life, football was beginning to feel like a job. It wasn't just that in Kansas City I was lifting weights for the first time in my career, and it wasn't just that our workdays were longer than they were in San Francisco. It was me. All of a sudden, I was dreading getting up in the morning and going to work. It didn't help that after five games, I had sore ribs and a bruised hip that made it too painful to practice.

*Playing against his old teammates,
and his quarterbacking heir Steve
Young, for the first and only time
in 1994, Montana leads his new*

"Joe brought the best out of everyone else. He lifted you to another level. He made you want to go make that big play, too."

JONATHAN HAYES,
TEAMMATE, KANSAS CITY CHIEFS

Naturally, I felt better on game days. In our sixth game, on Monday Night Football, we played Denver in Denver, and it was one of those classic games: Elway taking the Broncos up and down the field, and me taking the Chiefs. We threw eighty-three passes between us. After Elway's four-yard touchdown run put them ahead with a minute and a half to play, I had one more chance to overtake him.

It worked like magic. We went seventy-five yards in nine plays. I completed six of seven passes, most of them short, taking what they were giving us. The last one went to Willie Davis. He made a great catch at the goal line, heading toward the sideline, and drove into the end zone just inside the pylon. There were just eight seconds left to play. Not enough time even for Elway.

There weren't many moments left like that. Buffalo killed us in Buffalo. I was sacked three times, and Bruce Smith, who had given me that concussion in the AFC Championship Game, was hanging on me all day. One time, after he hit me, I walked over to Bruce and said, "I'm too old for this."

Not quite as defiant as when I told Too Tall Jones, "Respect that!"

We got our record to 7-4, then lost three straight games. I sprained my left foot in the first defeat, sat out the next two. I came back in time for victories over the Oilers and the Raiders that got us into the playoffs, just barely, as a wild-card team. In the game that knocked the Raiders out of the playoffs, Marcus Allen ran for 132 yards. I banged up my left knee, badly enough that I needed surgery after the season.

I played my final NFL game in the opening round of the playoffs against the Miami Dolphins. I guess my skills weren't completely gone. *The New York Times* said:

"The day began with a flawless Montana drive, eighty yards in eleven plays with Montana completing six passes in six attempts and baffling the Dolphins with play action that bordered on the sleight of hand when he hit Walker with a one-yard touchdown pass in the corner of the end zone."

The game did not end quite so well. We were losing, 27-17, early in the fourth quarter, but we had moved from our territory to the Miami five-yard line. I threw what was supposed to be a quick slant to Eric Martin, a quick touchdown, but for the first time all day, I was intercepted. A few minutes later, our season, and my career, was over.

"Most quarterbacks ask, 'What do I have to do to help us win?'
Joe asks, 'Who do I have to get the ball to, to help us win?'"

NICK LOWERY, TEAMMATE, KANSAS CITY CHIEFS

The jersey may change, but the legend remains the same:
The uniform Joe wore in his last game as an NFL player.

"He didn't end his career as a backup.
He didn't go out with a whimper.
He went out with a bang. He raised the
level of people around him in Kansas
City just as he did in San Francisco."

PAT HADEN, BROADCASTER AND EX-QUARTERBACK

December 31, 1994: After sixteen seasons, Joe Montana
is introduced in what would be his final NFL game.

**"My career was like living a dream.
Like all dreams, I woke up.
It's time to move on."**
JOE MONTANA

Montana with Nathaniel on Eddie DeBartolo's ranch in Montana.

It is almost impossible to measure Joe Montana's career purely in numbers, impressive as they are. He ranks among the top four quarterbacks in the history of the National Football League in passes attempted, passes completed, passing yardage, and touchdown passes. He is second in highest percentage of passes completed and in lowest percentage of passes intercepted. But the numbers only hint at the magnitude of his ability.

Montana is, in a sense, the football equivalent of Al Oerter, the great discus thrower who competed in four Olympic Games and won four Olympic gold medals, each time overcoming injury and winning literally with the best throw of his life. Of course Oerter had massive strength and stamina, and of course he was a master of technique, but what lifted him above all other Olympians was his heart, his reactions to pressure, his ability to raise his skills as the stakes rose.

Montana, too, brought the requisite physical and technical skills to his game—the quick feet, the strong arm (much stronger than people gave him credit for), the high threshold of pain essential to withstand persistent pounding, the knack of reading defenses, spotting secondary and tertiary receivers. But Montana also possessed that invisible quality that enabled him to treat the last ninety seconds of a Super Bowl exactly the same as he would treat any other ninety seconds. The significance of a situation never awed him, only consumed and inspired him.

Now the football games are behind him, and Joe Montana is ready to begin the rest of his life. He goes in well-armed, with a bright and beautiful wife, with four effervescent children, and with the knowledge, which he would never admit out loud, that he was the greatest quarterback in the history of football.

Jennifer faked me out completely. I had no idea that she had organized a retirement party for me.

She even put Eddie DeBartolo up to inviting me to join him and his wife for a family function. I told him I'd be glad to come. I'd do anything for him.

One evening early in May 1995, I met Eddie and his wife, Candy, at the Sir Francis Drake Hotel in San Francisco. We had a couple of drinks, then we got into their limousine to go to dinner. I was talking about horses with Candy and wondering whether I'd be asked to say anything at the DeBartolos' party. I really wasn't paying attention when we arrived at a place called The Flood Mansion.

I was talking to Eddie as we walked in, focusing on what he was saying, and when he said to me, "Well, have a good time," I couldn't figure out what he meant at first.

Then I looked around and the first person I saw was Carl Crawley, who coached me and the Monongahela Little Wildcats in Pop Warner football. Then I saw Jeff Petrucci, my quarterback coach in high school, and Nick DeCicco, my roommate at Notre Dame, and Steve DeBerg, whom I backed up in San Francisco, and Dave Krieg, who backed me up in Kansas City, and Bill Walsh and George Seifert and Sam Wyche and Paul Hackett and Mike Holmgren and Lamar Hunt and Ronnie Lott and Charles Haley and Jonathan Hayes, Huey Lewis and The News, all of my family, and so many more. It was "This Is Your Life" with a cast of hundreds.

John Taylor was there, reviving memories of The Drive, the last-minute touchdown that beat Cincinnati in the Super Bowl, and so was Dwight Clark, reviving memories of The Catch. I was glad to see George Seifert. I was glad to see everybody. I had no more grudges, no hard feelings.

It was a beautiful party—I don't know how Jennifer was able to plan everything and get everyone together without me getting even a little suspicious—and maybe the best part was that I didn't have a chance to think about it, to get nervous.

I was nervous before the big public farewell in San Francisco. That came a few weeks before the private party, and it was held outdoors in a downtown plaza. I had heard that there might be ten or twenty thousand people there, and when you're going to have to talk in front of that many people, you always feel a little fear. I'd rather face a blitz than face an audience. I asked Jennifer if she wanted to give my speech for me, and I was only half-kidding.

But, as it turned out, I enjoyed the ceremony. The crowd was larger than expected, maybe as many as thirty or forty thousand people, and hundreds of them were carrying banners and hundreds more were wearing 49ers jerseys with my number. I told them, "I really, truly never thought this day would ever come where I would say that word—retirement. But, unfortunately, it's here."

Bill Walsh was the master of ceremonies, and John Madden, the broadcaster, spoke, and they both said lovely things about me, and I was surrounded by teammates and friends and family and the fans who had embraced the 49ers in the 1980s. "This is the wake-up call for me," I told them. "It's time to move on."

The next day we had a smaller ceremony in Kansas City, at Arrowhead Stadium, and outside about a hundred fans stood and chanted, "One more year." Inside, I was really touched by how many of my teammates showed up, Marcus Allen and Neil Smith, Joe Valerio, Tim Grunhard, and Jonathan Hayes, to name a few, so many of the guys who had really

"... I didn't think I'd ever lose the passion or drive to compete in the NFL. When that happens, it's time to quit. I'm still healthy and relatively in one piece considering the game and how it's played. Now it's time to pull out the golf clubs."
JOE MONTANA

become good friends during my final two seasons. Coach Schottenheimer got all emotional. He had tears in his eyes when he talked about me. The Kansas City people will always be special to me. I just wish we had made it together to a Super Bowl.

Once again, I told everyone how hard it was for me to say the "R" word—retirement. I guess I was like most athletes: I thought I'd play forever. I thought I was indestructible, despite all the medical evidence to the contrary.

Some people thought that Jennifer had pushed me to retire, but that just wasn't true. Of course she was hoping that I would leave football before I suffered an injury that might affect the rest of my life, before my knees or my back or my brain got too banged up, but she knew that it had to be my choice, that I had to be ready to give it up.

And, finally, I was ready. I still had another year on my contract with the Chiefs, and if I had decided to play, I know I would have given it my best, but my heart just wasn't in it. The excitement wasn't there. I knew I was going to miss the games, the teammates, the challenge of something new every play, the endless variety of possibilities, but I wasn't going to miss the practices, the meetings, the weight room. Jennifer kept asking me, "Are you sure?" And I thought about it and I said I was.

Sports had been my life for almost all of my thirty-eight years, and I loved competitive sports, but I wanted to spend more time riding horses, fishing, getting my golf scores down, enjoying all the diversions I'd been too busy for.

"I couldn't believe how pumped up I got by the speed and power all around me. I really admired the drivers."
MONTANA AT INDIANAPOLIS 500 WITH THE CHIP GANASSI/TARGET RACING TEAM.

I thought about buying a thousand acres somewhere and building a family enclave, an area where Jennifer and I and the kids could live, and my Mom and Dad would have a home, and Jen's Mom and her brother and sister. I also thought about growing grapes in the Napa Valley, a small vineyard, not a big place, just big enough so that I could make wine for my family and for my friends. I wanted to travel, go to places in Europe and in Asia, where I wouldn't be recognized, where I wouldn't be in the spotlight. I once heard Michael Jordan tell someone who said he'd love to be him, "It's easy to be me for one day, but try being me for a year." I knew what he meant. Not to the same extent, of course, but enough. I wanted to see the sights and learn the history and the customs of the places I saw.

I thought one of the reasons I retired was to relax, to kick back and take it easy, but I may have to wait a few years for that. I couldn't believe how busy I was in the months after I announced the end of my football career. For one thing, I became involved in auto racing, as a partner in the Chip Ganassi/Target Racing Team, and I went out to Indianapolis, first for the time trials, and then for the 500 itself, and I couldn't believe how pumped up I got by the speed and the power all around me. I really admired the drivers. I don't know how they were able to concentrate, with people hovering over them all

the time. They didn't seem to have any fear. I think I might be tempted to race if I didn't have a wife and four children.

It's not the same as driving a race car, but I do get a big kick out of flying my own plane, a single-engine Malibu Mirage that Jen bought me as a present. It'll seat four passengers plus the pilot, and it's pressurized to 25,000 feet. I learned how to fly in 1991 and 1992, when I couldn't play and the 49ers didn't want me around as a distraction. I distracted myself with flying lessons, and I loved it. I got to fly with the Blue Angels once, and the pilot took me through a barrel roll—I can't tell you what a rush it was. I have to admit it's a little scary sometimes—landing in a strong wind will keep you alert—but I'm still learning. Sometimes when the instruments say that I'm flying level, I'll feel like I'm tilting to the right or to the left, and my instructor will tell me, "When you're up here, don't believe anything but the instruments. Don't believe what you feel. Don't even believe what I tell you. Just believe the instruments."

I also signed an agreement with NBC Sports to work on their studio show part-time during the NFL season. I'm looking forward to working with Greg Gumbel, who's a real professional, and Mike Ditka, who comes from Western Pennsylvania. I'm sure they'll bring me along slowly, like all my coaches did.

"When he's in the air, that's the only time he has that same glow as when he's playing football, maybe even a bigger glow. His eyes get really big, and they sparkle, and he talks about side winds, spin recovery, crosswind landings, and where he's flying to next. It'll never make up for playing the game, but it'll ease the emptiness." JENNIFER MONTANA

Following pages: *Montana pride: Nathaniel, Alexandra, Nicholas, and Elizabeth.*

I think I'll be able to bring something to broadcasting, an understanding of the thinking on the field, an understanding of the mentality of the players. And I hope players will trust me, will be a little more open with me, I guess, than I used to be with the media. I'm glad I'll have an excuse to be around football a while longer.

Most of all, I'm glad I'm going to have more time to be with my family, to be a full-time husband and daddy. Jennifer told me about the time a few years ago, when Alexandra was three or four years old and they were looking at photographs together, and Jen pointed to a picture of Alexandra and said, "Who's that?" and she said, "That's me." And then Jennifer pointed to a picture of me playing with Alexandra, and said, "Who's that?" and Alexandra said, "That's Daddy." And then Jennifer turned to a picture of me on the sidelines in my 49ers uniform and said, "Who's that?" and Alexandra said, "That's Joe Montana."

Now I'm Daddy, I'm not Joe Montana, and I'm going to be able to watch Alexandra and Elizabeth and Nathaniel and Nicholas grow up. The timing is perfect. When I retired they were all still under ten. I've never been very good at going to athletic events—I don't enjoy watching, I'd rather be playing—but when I went to one of Alexandra and Elizabeth's baseball games, pitching-machine games, I really

got excited, the first time I can remember getting excited as a spectator. I guess I acted like a 49ers fan, or a Chiefs fan. And I've enjoyed watching Nathaniel in his T-ball games; one of his little teammates was Nikolai Bonds, Barry Bonds' son. I enjoyed helping to coach the kids, playing catch with them or hitting fly balls.

I hope my children enjoy sports, but I'm not pushing them to be athletes. I know Alexandra would rather read a book, though she tries hard when she is playing, and that's all right with me. One of the reasons Jennifer and I chose our home is that it's close to good schools; we both try to emphasize the importance of education. On the invitation to my surprise retirement party, Jen listed nineteen reasons for me not to retire, and four of them were "Alexandra—Stanford. Elizabeth—Harvard. Nathaniel—Notre Dame. Nicholas—Princeton." She also listed nineteen reasons for me to retire. Number two was "Reggie White." Number eighteen was "Screw it, kids will have to get scholarships."

I feel like I've been on scholarship most of my life, and it's been a terrific ride. I've gone places, done things I couldn't have dreamed about when I was growing up in Monongahela. And my life's a long way from being over.

It's not even the end of the first half, and remember, I've always been at my best in the fourth quarter.

"This courtyard is kind of like a magical place for us both.
It's very Mediterranean, very Italian. So much a part of that feel
is the statues and fountains. It's one place where we like to eat or
just sit and read. It gets shaded in the afternoon, which makes it a really nice,
comfortable spot. The tranquil waters and the dripping fountain are so peaceful."
JENNIFER MONTANA

"Growing up I had a lot of those little two-wheeled mini bikes.
We used to run around in the backyards and out in the fields on them.
Now we have the go-cart and everyone wants to ride—it's a blast.
I like driving it as much as the kids do. If we had a couple of them
we could race, but I'm sure we'd end up crashing.
The whole family is very competitive."

JOE MONTANA

"'Camp Montana' just kind of evolved through the desire to keep our whole family active. With four kids, we're always trying to find new ways to keep them entertained and have fun. Jen started the girls rollerblading. I was just a goalie with my sneakers on at first, and the rest of them would skate around me. The first time I pulled on the rollerblades, I was scared to death. All I could see was me falling on

"We know we'll never be in a rodeo or showing any horses, but we're learning a lot and really enjoying it. This is definitely going to be part of what we visualize up in Napa. We like to kid Joe about looking forward to getting up in the morning and riding one of his horses down to check the grapes, with his fishing pole on his back, and then heading down to the pond or river to fish." JENNIFER MONTANA

"Ronnie Lott introduced us to Tae Kwon Do a couple of years back—
I wanted to be in top shape for the upcoming season with the Chiefs.
The key to these workouts is that it's something that you can have
fun with. Our instructor, George Chung, a Tae Kwon Do Master, is
always changing it for us, so when you get there you don't feel like
you're in the same humdrum place, doing the same program. It's the
hardest workout, the best all-around exercise and conditioning that
Jen and I have ever experienced." JOE MONTANA

"Cooking is my way of relaxing, and a chance for Jen and me to talk about what happened throughout the day. I try a few different things here and there, but I'm a pretty basic cook—I go for the old standards. Probably my all-time favorite would be my mother's ravioli. Jen makes such unbelievable pizzas and pastas and fresh sauces that I've been trying to talk her into opening a small restaurant. We both enjoy eating and we both enjoy cooking."
JOE MONTANA

Right: *Theresa Montana joins Joe and Jennifer in the family kitchen.*

"I'll tell you what I'd really like to do. I'd like to go up to northern California wine country, Napa or Sonoma, and settle down there. Open a little Italian restaurant with seven or eight or ten tables and a big wine list. I'd like to own some vineyard land, grow my own grapes, make wine."

JOE MONTANA

"It was a 1939 Spanish home, re-done in 'Early Linoleum' fifties style. From all our travels in Italy, we knew we wanted to make this home as close to a seventeenth-century Italian villa as we could with all the modern conveniences. We made three trips to France and Italy and brought back several containers of things, from bathtubs to fireplaces, just to complete the feel. We initially had planned to change about forty per cent of it and as it turned out, we changed about ninety-eight per cent of it. We love it."

JENNIFER MONTANA

"Sports has been very good to me. I've been very fortunate in terms of where I am and how I got here. Growing up around sports, you learn how to deal with people, in day-to-day life. There are certain rules to life, as there are to games, that put you in the position of learning that it's not my turn, it's his turn, and that in order to succeed we need to work together. These are valuable lessons.

The support that Jennifer's mom and my parents have given us throughout our lives has been instrumental in our success. If Jennifer and I can pass on those lessons and provide half of that support to our kids, I'd be very happy. You just hope that you give them a strong foundation, and one hopes that with the way things are going in the real world today, that we never, ever lose touch with who really gives support and where the real meaning of life comes from, and that's your family."

REGULAR SEASON

YEAR	TEAM		PASSING										RUSHING			
		G/S	ATT.	COMP.	YDS.	PCT.	TD	INT.	LG	RATING	NO.	YDS.	AVG.	LG	TD
1979	San Francisco	16/1	23	13	96	56.5	1	0	18	81.1	3	22	7.3	13	0
1980	San Francisco	15/7	273	176	1,795	64.5	15	9	71	87.8	32	77	2.4	11	2
1981	San Francisco	16/16	488	311	3,565	63.7	19	12	58	88.4	25	95	3.8	20	2
1982	San Francisco	9/9	346	213	2,613	61.6	17	11	55	88.0	30	118	3.9	21	1
1983	San Francisco	16/16	515	332	3,910	64.5	26	12	77	94.6	61	284	4.7	18	2
1984	San Francisco	16/15	432	279	3,630	64.6	28	10	80	102.9	39	118	3.0	15	2
1985	San Francisco	15/15	494	303	3,653	61.3	27	13	66	91.3	42	153	3.6	16	3
1986	San Francisco	8/8	307	191	2,236	62.2	8	9	48	80.7	17	38	2.2	17	0
1987	San Francisco	13/11	398	266	3,054	66.8	31	13	57	102.1	35	141	4.0	20	1
1988	San Francisco	14/13	397	238	2,981	59.9	18	10	96	87.9	38	132	3.5	15	3
1989	San Francisco	13/13	386	271	3,521	70.2	26	8	95	112.4	49	227	4.6	19	3
1990	San Francisco	15/15	520	321	3,944	61.7	26	16	78	89.0	40	162	4.1	20	1
1991*	San Francisco	—	—	—	—	—	—	—	—	—	—	—	—	—	—
1992	San Francisco	1/0	21	15	126	71.4	2	0	17	118.4	3	28	9.3	16	0
1993	Kansas City	11/11	298	181	2,144	60.7	13	7	50	87.4	25	64	2.6	17	0
1994	Kansas City	14/14	493	299	3,283	60.6	16	9	57	83.6	18	17	0.9	13	0
Totals		192/164	5,391	3,409	40,551	63.2	273	139	96	92.3	457	1,676	3.7	21	20

POST SEASON

YEAR	TEAM		PASSING										RUSHING			
		G/S	ATT.	COMP.	YDS.	PCT.	TD	INT.	LG	RATING	NO.	YDS.	AVG.	LG	TD
1981	San Francisco	3/3	88	56	747	63.6	6	4	58	94.4	12	4	0.3	7	1
1983	San Francisco	2/2	79	45	548	57.0	4	2	76	85.1	7	56	3.2	18	0
1984	San Francisco	3/3	108	67	873	62.0	7	5	40	89.9	13	144	11.1	53	1
1985	San Francisco	1/1	47	26	296	55.3	0	1	36	65.7	1	0	0.0	0	0
1986	San Francisco	1/1	15	8	98	53.3	0	2	24	34.2	0	0	0.0	0	0
1987	San Francisco	1/1	26	12	109	46.2	0	1	33	42.0	3	20	6.7	14	0
1988	San Francisco	3/3	90	56	823	62.2	8	1	61	117.0	11	39	3.5	11	0
1989	San Francisco	3/3	83	65	800	78.3	11	0	72	146.4	5	19	3.8	10	0
1990	San Francisco	2/2	57	40	464	70.2	3	1	61	104.7	3	10	3.3	6	0
1992*	San Francisco	—	—	—	—	—	—	—	—	—	—	—	—	—	—
1993	Kansas City	3/3	104	59	700	56.7	4	3	41	78.2	6	13	2.2	7	0
1994	Kansas City	1/1	37	26	314	70.3	2	1	57	102.8	2	5	2.5	7	0
Totals		23/23	734	460	5,772	62.7	45	21	76	95.3	63	310	4.9	53	2

LEGEND

G/S	GAMES/STARTER	PCT.	COMPLETION PERCENTAGE	RATING	QUARTERBACK RATING
ATT.	ATTEMPTS	TD	TOUCHDOWNS	NO.	NUMBER OF RUSHES
COMP.	COMPLETIONS	INT.	INTERCEPTIONS	AVG.	AVERAGE GAIN
YDS.	TOTAL YARDS	LG	LONGEST GAIN	LG	LONGEST GAIN

*DID NOT PLAY DUE TO INJURY.

The memories live on: Mementos from the Montana trophy case.

RECORD AS A STARTER
(Regular Season)

TEAM	W	L
Atlanta	14	5
Buffalo	3	2
Chicago	3	3
Cincinnati	4	0
Cleveland	4	1
Dallas	4	0
Denver	2	4
Detroit	1	3
Green Bay	3	1
Houston	5	0
Indianapolis	1	0
Kansas City	2	0
L.A. Raiders	4	2
L.A. Rams	12	8
Miami	0	2
Minnesota	3	2
New England	4	0
New Orleans	15	2
N.Y. Giants	4	1
N.Y. Jets	1	1
Philadelphia	1	1
Phoenix/St. Louis	4	1
Pittsburgh	2	2
San Diego	3	3
San Francisco	1	0
Seattle	5	1
Tampa Bay	7	1
Washington	5	1
Totals	**117**	**47**

SINGLE GAME CAREER HIGHS
(includes Playoffs)

Pass Attempts: 60 vs. Washington, 11/17/86
Pass Completions: 37 vs. Atlanta, 10/06/85
Passing Yards: 476 vs. Atlanta, 10/14/90
Touchdown Passes: 6 vs. Atlanta, 10/14/90
Interceptions: 4 vs. Cincinnati, 11/04/84
Long Pass: 96 (to Jerry Rice) vs. San Diego, 11/27/88
Rushing Attempts: 9 vs. Tampa Bay, 09/17/89
Rushing Yards: 63 vs. N.Y. Giants, 12/29/84
Touchdown Runs: 1, 22 times
Long Run: 53 yards vs. N.Y. Giants, 12/29/84
Times Sacked: 8 vs. L.A. Rams, 12/18/88 and
vs. Philadelphia, 09/24/88

REGULAR SEASON TD TARGETS

RECEIVER	TD'S
Jerry Rice	55
Dwight Clark	41
Freddie Solomon	29
Roger Craig	15
John Taylor	15
Russ Francis	12
Mike Wilson	12
Brent Jones	9
Earl Cooper	8
Willie Davis	8
John Frank	8
Wendell Tyler	6
Charle Young	6
J. J. Birden	5
Jeff Moore	4
Renaldo Nehemiah	4
Tom Rathman	4
Marcus Allen	3
Keith Cash	3
Ron Heller	3
Eason Ramson	3
Joe Valerio	3
Lake Dawson	2
Mike Sherrard	2
Derrick Walker	2
Kimble Anders	1
Bob Bruer	1
Lenvil Elliott	1
Tracy Greene	1
Jonathan Hayes	1
Amp Lee	1
Guy McIntyre	1
Carl Monroe	1
Ricky Patton	1
Bill Ring	1
Harry Sydney	1
Totals	**273**

COMEBACKS

Joe Montana has engineered 31 fourth-quarter comebacks in his illustrious NFL career. The following is a list of games in which Montana brought the 49ers (26 times) and Chiefs (5 times) back from fourth-quarter deficits to dramatic wins:

DATE	OPPONENT	END OF 3RD QUARTER SCORE	FINAL SCORE
12/07/80	New Orleans [7]	21-35	38-35
11/01/81	at Pittsburgh	10-14	17-14
11/22/81	at L.A. Rams [1]	27-24	33-31
01/10/82	Dallas [2]	21-27	28-27
12/02/82	at L.A. Rams [1]	20-17	30-24
12/26/82	at Kansas City	9-10	26-13
09/25/83	Atlanta	17-20	24-20
10/23/83	at L.A. Rams	17-28	45-35
12/31/83	Detroit [3]	17-23	24-23
09/02/84	at Detroit	17-20	30-27
11/04/84	Cincinnati	10-17	23-17
12/15/85	at New Orleans	17-19	31-19
12/14/86	at New England	16-17	29-24
09/20/87	at Cincinnati	20-26	27-26
10/18/87	at St. Louis	21-28	34-28
10/25/87	at New Orleans	17-19	24-22
09/11/88	at N.Y. Giants	13-17	20-17
10/16/88	at L.A. Rams	17-21	24-21
01/22/89	Cincinnati [4]	6-13	20-16
08/17/89	at Tampa Bay	6-9	20-16
09/24/89	at Philadelphia	10-21	38-28
11/06/89	at New Orleans	10-17	24-20
12/11/89	at L.A. Rams	10-24	30-27
09/10/90	at New Orleans [1]	10-9	13-12
10/07/90	at Houston	14-21	24-21
12/10/90	at Cincinnati [1, 7]	14-10	20-17
10/17/93	at San Diego	7-10	17-14
01/08/94	Pittsburgh [5, 7]	10-17	27-24
01/16/94	at Houston [6]	7-10	28-20
10/17/94	at Denver [1]	21-21	31-28
11/20/94	Cleveland	10-13	20-13

[1] team fell behind during fourth quarter
[2] NFC Championship Game
[3] NFC Divisional Playoff Game
[4] Super Bowl XXIII
[5] AFC First Round Playoff Game
[6] AFC Divisional Playoff Game
[7] overtime game

NFL LEADERS

CAREER QUARTERBACK RATING
(Minimum 1,500 Attempts)

1. Steve Young, 1985–	96.8
2. Joe Montana, 1979–94	92.3
3. Dan Marino, 1983–	88.2
4. Jim Kelly, 1986–	85.8
5. Roger Staubach, 1969–79	83.4

CAREER PASSING YARDS

1. Fran Tarkenton, 1961–78	47,003
2. Dan Marino, 1983–	45,173
3. Dan Fouts, 1973–87	43,040
4. Joe Montana, 1979–94	40,551
5. John Elway, 1983–	37,736

CAREER PASSING TOUCHDOWNS

1. Fran Tarkenton, 1961–78	342
2. Dan Marino, 1983–	328
3. Johnny Unitas, 1954–73	290
4. Joe Montana, 1979–	273
5. Sonny Jurgensen, 1957–74	255

CAREER PASS COMPLETIONS

1. Fran Tarkenton, 1961–78	3,686
2. Dan Marino, 1983–	3,604
3. Joe Montana, 1979–94	3,409
4. Dan Fouts, 1973–87	3,297
5. John Elway, 1983–	3,030

CAREER PASS ATTEMPTS

1. Fran Tarkenton, 1961–78	6,467
2. Dan Marino, 1983–	6,049
3. Dan Fouts, 1973–87	5,604
4. Joe Montana, 1979–94	5,391
5. John Elway, 1983–	5,384

CAREER REGULAR SEASON VICTORIES
(As a Starter)

1. Fran Tarkenton, 1961–78	125
2. Johnny Unitas, 1954–73	119
3. Joe Montana, 1979–94	117

STATISTICAL APPENDIX COMPILED BY NATIONAL FOOTBALL
LEAGUE PROPERTIES, INC.

ACKNOWLEDGMENTS

OPUS PRODUCTIONS INC.

President/Creative Director: Derik Murray
Designer: Dave Mason/Dave Mason & Associates
Production Manager: Paula Guise
Design/Production Assistant:
Pamela Lee/Dave Mason & Associates
Visual Coordinator: Anne Boa
Assistant Visual Coordinator: Joanne Powers
Artifact Photography Producer: Andreanne Ricard
Artifact Photography: Derik Murray Photography
Inc./Brad Stringer, Jason Stroud, with the assistance
of Bill Faulkner

Vice President, Sales and Marketing: Glenn McPherson
Marketing Coordinator: David Attard

Vice President/Publishing Director: Marthe Love
Coauthor: Dick Schaap
Editor: Brian Scrivener
Editorial Coordinator: Wendy Darling
Editorial Assistant: Robin Evans
Project Accountant: Kim Steele
In-house Counsel: Ruth Chang
Executive Assistant: Barbara Talbot
Reception: Lana Thomas

Opus Productions would like to thank the following:
IMG: Peter Johnson, Cheryl Tate, Karin Arnold,
Karen Newark

Turner Publishing, Inc.: Michael Reagan, Walton
Rawls, Michael Walsh, Nancy Robins, William
Muller, Marshall Orson, Bee Espy, Tom Maiellaro,
Lauren Emerson, Marty Moore, Michon Wise

National Football League Properties, Inc.: John
Weibusch, Paul Spinelli, Kevin Terrell, Matt Marini

Treasure trove: Theresa and Joseph Montana's scrapbook from Joe, Jr.'s Ringgold years.

*Opus Productions would like to extend a special thank you to the Montana family: Joe, for his dedication and uncompromising
enthusiasm in sharing his life in words and pictures; Jennifer, for her beautiful photographs and warm hospitality; Joe, Sr. and Theresa,
for sharing their memories and family archives; to Alexandra, Elizabeth, Nathaniel, and Nicholas, for their spirited cooperation;
and Elinor Johnson, for generously providing her collection of photographs and memorabilia.*

Opus Productions would like to acknowledge the following for their assistance and support:
Kelly Chapman • Dwight Clark, Angel Mejia, Clark's by the Bay • Jeanne Collins • Edward J. DeBartolo, Jr., San Francisco 49ers • Greg della Stua, PrintNet
• James F. Dougherty II • Trevor Doull, Sportsbook Plus • Stephen Fane • Andrew Fink, National Football League • Gord Forbes • John Hamilton
• John Heisler, Jaime Owen Cripe, University of Notre Dame • Lamar Hunt, Susie Napoli, Kansas City Chiefs • Walter Iooss, Jr. • Del Litle, Inland Press
• Candace and Quinn Mason • Betty Murray • Devin and Taylor Murray • Gene Nemitz • Cliff Pickles • Peter Scarth, Kodak Canada • Jeremy Schaap
• Maria Sota, Digital PrePress International • Heintz Kleutmeier, Karen Carpenter, Mike Dickson, *Sports Illustrated* • Jeff Thomlinson • Dean Tutor, LA Gear
• RobinVan Heck • Margalo Whyte • Michael Zagaris • Paul Zolak, Ringgold High School • All artifacts photographed exclusively on Ektachrome Professional film.

PHOTOGRAPHY CREDITS
Cover: **Albert Watson** • Montana family photo session: **Walter Iooss, Jr.**
Boss, Dave/NFL Photos: 75 above; **Carlick, Jeff**/Sportschrome/East West: 79; **Clarkson, Rich**: 32; **Desprois, Dennis**/NFL Photos: 46; **Dipace, Tom**: 89, 102;
Flores, Art: 118; **Fogel, Ric**/Bernhardt Sport Photos: 105; **Greule, Otto**/ALLSPORT: 81 right; **Hayt, Andy**/NFL Photos; 75 below; **Hayt, Andy**/*S.I.*: 61, 66;
Hathaway, Steve: 65; **Iooss Jr., Walter**: 4, 114, 115, 116/117, 119, 120/121, 122, 123, 124, 125, 126, 127, 128, 129, 130, 131, 132, 133, 134, 135, 136, 137;
Iooss, Jr., Walter/ *S.I.*: 15 below, 30; **Iwasaki, Carl**/*S.I.*: 15 above; Courtesy of **Elinor Johnson**: 2, 17, 18, 23; **Kane, Rich**/Sportschrome/East West: 81 left;
Kee, Allen/Bob Rosato Sport Photography: 94; **Leifer, Neil**/*S.I.*: 35; **Mackson, Richard**/*S.I.*: 83; **Maniello, Vincent**/Sportschrome/East West: 100; **McDonough,
John**/NFL Photos: 56/57, 60, 76/77; **McDonough, John**/*S.I.*: 78; **Messerschmidt, Al**: 97; **Messerschmidt, Al**/NFL Photos: 62/63; **Miller, Peter Read**: 86, 144;
Miller, Peter Read/NFL Photos: 71; **Miller, Peter Read**/*S.I.*: 111; **Montana, Jennifer**: 110, 138, back endsheet; Courtesy of **Theresa Montana**: front endsheet,
20, 21, 22, 28, 34, back cover; **Mount, Bill**/NFL Photos: 108/109; **Pfleger, Mickey**/Sports California: 7, 8, 11, 12, 54, 55, 59, 80, 112; **Powell, Mike**/ALLSPORT:
98; **Powell, Mike**/NFL Photos: 48; **Raymond, Joe**: 36, 38/39, 41, 42; **Reece, Kevin**: 96; Courtesy of **Ringgold High School**: 24/25; **Rose, George**/NFL Photos 67;
Courtesy of **Schick**: 64; **Tielemans, Al**/*S.I.*: 104; **Tringali, Jr., Rob**/Sportschrome/East West: 95; Courtesy of **University of Notre Dame**: 29, 40; **Watson, Albert**: cover;
Woltmann, Steve: 90; **Young, Hank**/Young Co.: 92/93, 103, 106; **Zagaris, Michael**: 10, 13, 45, 49, 50, 51, 52, 53, 56 left, 58, 68, 69, 72, 73, 74, 87;
Zagaris, Michael/NFL Photos: 84.
S.I. = Sports Illustrated

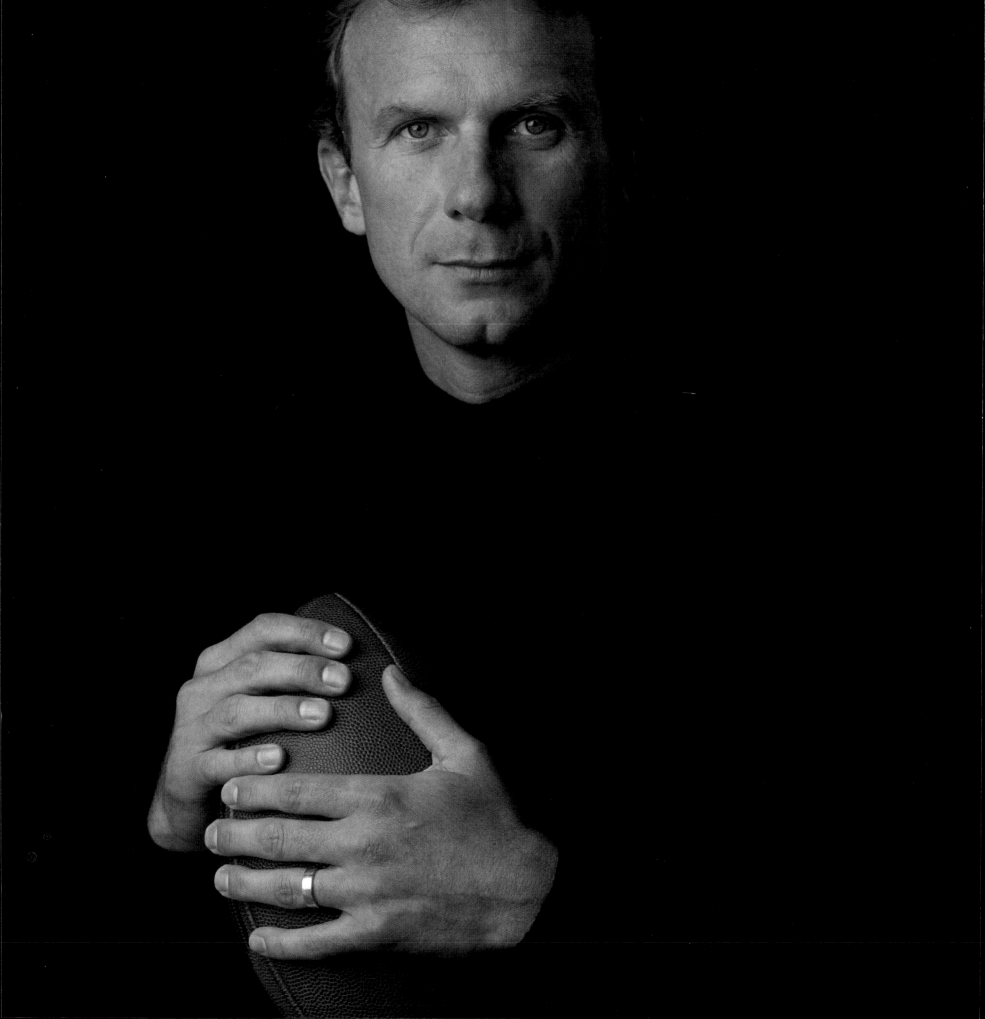